how to start a home-based

Car Detailing Business

Renny Doyle

gpp ®

Guilford, Connecticut

Copyright © 2012 by Morris Book Publishing, LLC

Editorial Director: Cynthia Hughes Cullen
Editor: Tracee Williams
Project Editor: Lauren Brancato
Text Design: Sheryl P. Kober
Layout: Sue Murray

Library of Congress Cataloging-in-Publication Data is available on file.

ISBN 978-0-7627-7876-8

Printed in the United States of America

10 9 8 7 6 5 4 3 2 1

Thanks to the Lord above for always loving me. My wife, Diane, and my kids, Ryan, Devin, Dalaney, and Daryn, you make life sweet. Mom and Nana, my three brothers, and the best group of friends a man could have, thanks for all the support and love. McKinley dog, I built my business with you by my side and I sure miss you, buddy.

Contents

Acknowledgments

I am a blessed man to do in life what many do as a hobby. Getting to this point was not an easy process nor was the road without bumps. I could have never arrived where I am today without the love, support, and help of many.

The good Lord above has gifted me with the ideal group of family, friends, clients, and coworkers, and a great network of amazing professionals. I will start with the publishing team for this book. Tracee Williams, development/project editor with Globe Pequot Press, thank you for all the help, instruction, support, and input. You turned this crusty detailer into a writer and I appreciate all your hard work.

Going way back, I want to thank my buddy Vonhotrod and his dad for getting me into the car-show gig back in the '80s. Von, you and your dad took a passion and started it on fire! To my many clients over the years, especially Dave Morris who is now like family. Bill Bartel, the late Art Scholl, Evan Elliott, and Aeroshell (Jerry and Paul), thank you for not only believing in me, but for building me up and allowing me the chance to work on some amazing aircraft and cars over the years. You guys laid the foundation of success for me. Walt and Monique, you got me here and I could not have two better friends or mentors. You two are family and I love you both dearly. Mr. Johnson, you are far more than a teacher, you are a life saver. When few had belief in me, you did.

To all my detailing buddies, especially those who contributed to this book, I thank you for the mentorship and friendship over the years. To the Detailing Mafia, you all make my life and my work far more enjoyable.

Dad, I thank you for giving me the car-crazy bug. This passed-along gene is not just a trait that I love, it's my lifestyle and I am sure it came directly from you. Life has given me three brothers who were always open to sharing and loving, and you three are not only brothers, but buddies. Rick, we have had a ton of adventure and fun, and I sure love you, bro! Randy, my brother, the most important gift you have given me is your special love and support. You have always been there for me. For a big brother to treat a little brother with such care and love has helped me be the man I am today. Big brother, I love you for being so uniquely you. Jerry, you are an adrenaline pill of life. Have we had fun or what? Just think, we are only at the halfway point and still alive to talk about it. Here's to many more dive-and-ski trips, bro.

While you may not be here with us directly, Nana, thank you for helping Mom raise me. You were the best friend a guy could ask for, and to have you as a grandma was far more than an honor. As you said to me many times, "UNA vita d'amore!"

Mom, we never had much money when I was growing up, but what we lacked in money we had in love. How you put up with me I will never understand but you were a friend, a dad, and the best mom a guy could have, all wrapped into one. I love you for showing me that true wealth has nothing to do with money and everything to do with the people we call family and friends. I love you, Mom.

My wife, Diane, you are a giving woman and thank you for joining me on this ride. It hasn't always been a smooth one and I appreciate your love and support, and for understanding the long hours and the time away from you. You are my dream girl, Di, and I love the life we have, baby. My car-crazy daughter Ryan, for being my car-show buddy. You and I share a car bug and bond that will never end. Devin, my son, you gave up many sporting events to join me at car and aircraft events when I am sure you would have rather been with your buddies. You are an ideal son, Dev! Dalaney Ruth, your life has never known me not detailing. You have been a champion about going to events, and I love you for it. I am thankful to have a daughter as cool as you, Dalaney. Daryn Vacco Doyle, you are one crazy kid and we have many years of cruising ahead of us.

I love you all and thank each of you for being so wonderful while I was writing this book. You are my world and I thank God for giving me the gift of you—my family and friends.

Introduction: Something for YOU to Think About

Just the fact that you picked up this book or searched it online is most likely due to one or more of these reasons:

- You have a passion for automobiles (maybe even planes, boats, and motorcycles, too).
- You desire to kick your boss to the curb and start your own gig.
- You are at a crossroads in life and need to reevaluate your career choice.
- You want to own your own business and are evaluating the detailing industry.

You and I are lucky. We are interested in an industry where we can enjoy our passion and make a living from it. Like you, I have worked for others and I am guessing that you WANT OUT of the eight-to-five rat race. I wanted out so badly I could taste it, and I could not wait for the day to **fire my boss.**

Like you, I wanted to make my own way in life and own my time. Like you, getting a vehicle clean and shiny offers instant gratification. I liked the feeling I had when I got the shine going on my own car, so why not get the feeling all the time and get paid for it?

By reading up on detailing, your goal is to learn about the industry so you can make smart decisions, right? My goal in this book is to not only educate you on the real facts about detailing, but to also keep you from making costly mistakes and wasting your valuable time. For as many truths as there are about the detailing industry, you can count on at least that many fairy tales.

The US Department of Commerce supplies data that tell a valuable story about small businesses today. They show that seven out of ten new businesses will not be in business five to ten years after they started. Which means you better know what you are doing and use every competitive advantage you can find to make sure you are not a statistic.

Throughout the book you will find profiles of professional detailers and business professionals called "To Do It All Over Again" and "What I Wish I Had Known Before I Started My Business." I think you will enjoy what these professionals have to say, as you can learn a great deal from those who have traveled the high and low roads of owning a business.

I am not an author being paid to write a book about detailing, I am a Master Level Detailer sharing my thirty-plus years of operating both small and large detailing operations, and by reading this book, you will gain valuable insights into the industry.

Starting a Detailing Business

So you want to start a business and, more specifically, a detailing business. I am gonzo, wacko, and completely crazy and passionate about detailing. The cool thing is that the passion I have for detailing could only be matched by you—someone as passionate about this idea now as I was many years ago when I started my business.

I am going to challenge you and I hope excite you in this book, and maybe even make you a little mad due to some of my blunt comments, but don't get angry, get motivated. Take a real hard look at the items I challenge you with. Dig deep into those challenges, as you have so much to both gain and lose.

Starting your own business is a challenge, and every business within every industry has its own particular pitfalls. Detailing also has its own higher-than-average niche markets that many mistakenly miss when entering or expanding within detailing.

My primary intentions in this book are directed at confirming that the dream of owning and running a detailing business can be real. One of my goals is to lead you around the pitfalls and directly to the signs and channels that other detailing professionals have looked for, developed, and succeeded in.

When a detailing business is started, planned for, and run properly, there are many factors that constantly make it a growth-based business: the soaring cost of new automobiles; the fact that people are buying higher-end vehicles; and that people are keeping their vehicles longer. These are the leading elements that contribute to the market value of a truly professional detailer. Also, detailing is a comfort business, meaning that our services make customers' lives easier and thus they become accustomed to our services as a regular part of their lives.

The detailing industry is currently seeing increased interest from people in other professions seeking out detailing as a possible business. Why?

- People today are looking to own their own time and to live the dream of a self-sustaining way of life. Detailing can offer a solid business while providing a life filled with what you want, not what your boss wants.
- Detailing is an affordable business to start, with average start-up costs being as low as a few thousand dollars.
- The days of twenty-five year careers within corporate America are nearly a thing of the past. People are looking for a way out of the rat race and into the freedom that owning a small business can offer.

This book is a true step-by-step guide on how to plan, structure, and build your business from the ground up. More importantly, it's about how to be profitable within your detailing business. No matter whether you are brand new to detailing or a seasoned veteran, this book will provide information that top-level detailers across the globe utilize.

Grab a highlighter and page tabs and mark, highlight, and flag the areas that peak your interest. A good book is a marked-up and heavily used book, and this book is a guide you will hopefully use for the life of your business and refer to over the years.

Ask Yourself: What Is Your Why? Why Start a Small Business?

Why start a detailing business? Do a little mind mapping (see details on the following page) by actually writing down what you are thinking—why you believe you are right for detailing, and why detailing is right for you. I want you to take a pen or pencil and do the exercises on page 3. Don't do this on your computer. A pen to paper has a better way of sticking in your brain and makes you truly think more.

Just like your life, a detailing business has chapters. Each chapter starts depending on where you are in life.

If you are young and just starting, you are far more able to put the hours into your business. You can cram, work hard, and dedicate a ton of hours to your business, and the rewards can be rapid.

Maybe you are like me, a parent who wants to enjoy his kids and not work a traditional job. Maybe you are at the end of your career and thinking of the "what's next" step in life. If you are one of these individuals, you will need to use your time

Top Five Reasons Why You Are Looking to Start a Detailing Business

Use this worksheet to write down your reasons.

1. _____

2. _____

3. _____

4. _____

5. _____

Mind Mapping

Learn more about mind mapping and how I use it within business by visiting my website www.detailingsuccess.com, and by searching the term "mind mapping." Mind mapping is a wonderful tool when you are building a business. I have also included a sample of one of my own mind-mapping sessions.

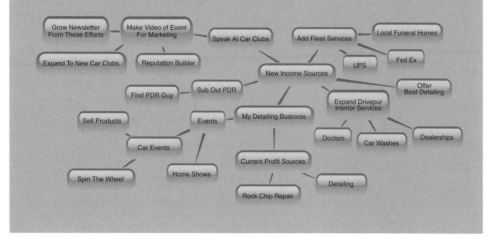

wisely. You will need to put in the hours—and I am going to be blunt—that even as a dad, I put in the "seat time," as race-car drivers say. I was up before my family and working after they went to bed. Don't rob your family of their time with you, work when they sleep. You can perform much of your marketing, bookkeeping, and equipment maintenance during early morning or late night. Building a business, any business, is going to take a large amount of your time. You will have to pay the price, and in the early days it can and will take a heavy toll. Don't make your family pay or you will lose more than just a business. Keep God, family, life, friends, and your health first.

Who Makes a Good Detailer?

If you consider yourself a car guy or car girl, this is one of the leading traits that indicate detailing might be right for you. I find that those who have a love affair with vehicles have a greater drive for success than those who don't.

Detailing is a heck of a lot more than just slapping some wax on a car. Truth be known, proper detailing can be very hard work. Here are some of the successful traits of great detailers I know. They:

- Understand that detailing without good business skills is a weakness that needs to be addressed.
- Realize that detailing is hard, physical work and that to operate at the top levels, one needs to be in good physical shape and stay healthy.
- Know that pro-level detailing requires outstanding people skills.
- Commit to long-term dedication and recognize that building a successful business takes time, as does building a solid set of detailing skills.
- Have a never-give-up attitude and know that success has no room for quitters.
- Are comfortable using power tools.
- Engage in learning new skills and continuing education.

One of the most difficult talents a true pro-level detailer can have is a good eye. This is far more important than being able to see a clean or dirty car. It includes being able to recognize:

- **Paint Defects**—Being able to clearly see and identify defects is harder than you may think. Not everyone has the eye for proper paint. In reality, the most money to be made within detailing is from the more common services. While a proper eye is important, what you can learn from a detailing artist will assist you most in developing your detailing eyes.
- **Proper Paint**—Give me one minute with a car and I can tell you if it's factory paint or a re-paint. Having an eye for detail is important and could keep you from damaging paint or being blamed for imperfections that were not your fault.
- **Interior Imperfections**—An eye for stains and what the expectations of the client are is an important factor to successful detailers. For some customers stains are not a big deal while for others the smallest remaining stain is a monumental issue. For instance, I am a stain snob and when I have checked out my competition, stains around the seat bases drive me nuts. I wonder why they would leave such an eyesore.

Hustle

One of the key elements you need in business is the ability, desire, and drive to hustle. If you can't hustle, keep your day job because without it, you are going to suck the wind right out of your business. I view myself as a true detailing professional and I rub elbows with some amazing clients and detailing professionals all over the world. Do you think that just happened? I hustled, worked, and sweat long hours, and performed untold hours of testing, practice, and research.

Hurry Up and Wait

Let me tell you, I wanted to succeed and needed to succeed as quickly as possible, but I knew that building my dream detailing empire would take time. Here is what I did:

- I spoke with everyone and anyone, and told them about my business.
- I used online opportunities to market my company's brand and my own personal brand. The web is amazing and be glad you live in today's technology-savvy world because it is much easier for those who get it and do it.
- I went into niches right off the bat and specialized in services that others within my markets were unable to perform or performed with terrible results.
- I invested in education.
- I studied the behavior of buyers and read extensively to become a professional salesperson.
- I spoke at small events and got people talking, then spoke at larger events and got more people talking. I have been mentioned in the *Wall Street Journal* and *Reader's Digest,* and on NPR Radio. These mentions can help bring in the $1,000, $5,000 and even $35,000 detail gigs.

Moral of the Story?

You gotta hustle to make it.
You gotta be patient to survive.

Patience

Another key element is patience. Building a business and a sustainable brand does not come instantly. I meet and talk with those looking to get into the business because they think it's easy. And if they are planning to make $10, $12, $15 an hour, they are right. Hitting the real money at $40 to $200 an hour takes time.

Passion Is a Giant Killer

How much do you want this business? I mean really want it? Can you taste the need? Will you immerse yourself in it? I can tell you that there are two major elements that will drive you to success, and passion is the first and most important. Developing a strong, educated business mind is next. Not everyone is born with a brilliant business mind, but if you are dedicated, you can evolve into the great mind it will take to succeed. I have seen some amazing business minds enter detailing and fail. Why? They didn't have a drop of passion for what they were doing, while others who were passionate as hell developed their business abilities and won big.

Let's face it, detailing the minivan of a busy mom with messy toddlers is not fun. And if you're not passionate about detailing, well, good luck. Passion will get you to the launch of your business. Passion will leapfrog you over others and it will carry you to success. Your passion will drive you no matter if you are working on the minivan from hell, or the finest Ferrari money can buy.

Passion will also carry you through the good and the bad, the highs and the lows, and it will separate you from average detailers. Passion is the edge that most fail to grasp and, more importantly, what even fewer have outright. When someone with extreme passion dives into detailing, their drive for success is difficult to match or beat.

Later in the book, we will be talking about some of the most common challenges within a detailing business and how true, bone-deep passion can help you hurdle the challenges you may face.

Of every tool you could have, and with all the education you could possibly gain, nothing—I repeat, nothing—beats passion. Just like a building, passion is only one element but it's the strongest and most powerful foundation you have within your DNA.

Now, passion unbridled is just passion with no direction. If you combine passion with knowledge, and add in business abilities, personality, and detailing talents, it will win many battles for you and take you far with the business you start. **Passion wins battles and builds success.**

Some Watch Things Happen, Some Make Things Happen, While Others Wonder What Happened

A never-quit attitude is a major element that will drive you to success. Dedication "wins wars." When I think of who makes a good detailer, I think of the movie *Rudy*. This movie was based on a true story about a young man who wished to play football for the great Notre Dame Fighting Irish. Rudy had many obstacles in his life that would make the average young man quit before he even got started.

Rudy was five-foot nothing and a hundred-and-nothing pounds, yet he kept working hard and would never give up. In the end, Rudy was one of the only players in school history to be carried off the field in celebration. Had he listened to his own family, friends, and coaches, he would have never realized his dream of being a Fighting Irish player. You will need that same level of dedication to become a successful detailer.

For the few who have done their homework and have made their decisions based on sound information, even if you have struggles or the timing is not absolutely perfect, as Rudy could tell you, where there is a will, there is a way.

Passion is energy. Feel the power that comes from focusing on what excites you.

—*Oprah Winfrey*

Do You Need Incredible Skills to be a Detailer?

The facts of professional detailing cover a wide spectrum of truths versus myths. Detailers are not born, they are developed and refined. I have trained, coached, and mentored a wide variety of people from twenty-year veterans of detailing to those who have never touched a power tool before.

Detailing skills can be learned but a poor work ethic is hard to change. I can teach most people the essentials of detailing, but I can't change laziness or an attitude of entitlement. No one is going to give you this business. You are going to need to earn every penny and each step of success you realize.

You may have never touched a polisher before, and that is okay, as that can be learned. On the flip side, I have witnessed people come into the detailing industry and perform at skill levels that were unbelievable, yet struggle to make a dime.

In turn, I have worked with others who were mediocre in skills yet understood the business, marketing, and sales aspects of their business, and soared to success.

This last group usually has one special trait in common: They are almost always very likable, energetic people with great people skills who also happen to understand what their detailing marketplace is looking for. Let's face it, within most markets, most people buying professional-level detail services are not having their vehicles wet dry or wet sanded, compounded, polished, and finished to a show-car finish. Most paying for detailing services simply desire a high-quality polish with a nice, long-lasting paint protection product applied to the exterior. Most detailing clients want an interior that is nice and clean with the spots and odors removed. A smart detailing business owner knows this and can profit in most cases without the need for skills that take a decade to develop.

> **Detailer Tip**
>
> Pro-level detailing has a certain level of skill that is needed no matter how basic the services you are offering. Being educated within detailing is not an option, it's a must. Just like doctors, dentists, or electricians, we detailers need to know our stuff! Think about that and plan on how you are going to become detailing smart.

Young versus Old

Many of the individuals I see entering the detailing industry today are middle aged, in their late thirties to late fifties, and I am asked all the time, how old is too old to start a detailing business? It depends on many factors.

Pro-level detailing can kick your butt. It's not easy work even when done with the latest and greatest tools and products. Detailing is hard physical work and you older people need to take this into consideration.

Now, with the reality clauses out of the way, let me be direct: You are never too old to detail as long as you are a "young" old guy or gal. I have people I work with who are near sixty and can work circles around many detailers that are in their twenties. Some people remain young longer than others and some have work ethics that could kill a water buffalo. Age is more than a number, it's an attitude and your own personal conditioning and life experiences will determine if you can handle detailing full or part time.

I work with people between the ages of forty-five and sixty all the time and if you are fit (or becoming fit again), have a youthful outlook, and share a passion for detailing cars, my money is on you. "Mature detailers," as I call them, happen to be some of the most profitable per-hour detailers I work with. Mature detailers have some direct advantages, one being life experience. The older crowd may not be as fast, nor as hip, but when it comes to having a true eye for detailing, the older crowd is pretty skilled and able.

Now let's beat up on the young studs for a while. I was young when I got into this game, and I was both stupid and lucky at the same time. I was all-knowing, but only for a short time. I met four very important people in my life who became my first mentors, and they were tough on me and kicked my butt, and a much-needed butt kicking it was. I learned to listen to these "old guys" but not until after I had fallen several times in business, and had some self-inflicted wounds all caused from my youthful ignorance.

- Art Scholl was the first to get me into detailing. This aviation pioneer, who died during the filming of the famed movie *Top Gun,* was a man's man and his impact on my early teen years was undeniably one of the key reasons I have the detailing bug today. He impacted me in a way that set me on a course of success. When I was just thirteen and randomly hanging out at the local small airport, Art approached me one day and asked, "Why don't you learn to fly, kid?" As a kid with little money, Art took to me and, in trade for me washing and waxing small aircraft, he taught me how to fly. That one chance meeting that one summer day set me on a direct course to become the detailer I am today, but yet another great man, Bill Bartel, cultivated the passion Art set in motion and put it into high gear.
- Bill Bartel entered my life during my teen years when I was just starting my detailing efforts. Bill's impact had little to do with detailing, even if I did detail his aircraft and cars. His real value in my life came as a man of God who had faults but admitted those faults. Bill is a smart, smart business-man, and his life caught my attention. He has always been a hard worker and shared with me his wonderful business mind, which I picked nonstop. Bill was instrumental in building the entrepreneurial foundation in my life, along with teaching me how to become a wise man, son, husband, and father. In great part, I am the man I am today due to Bill.
- Walt and Monique Stanckiewitz made one of the largest impacts on my life. This dynamic duo gave me many life lessons, but the most valuable one I gained from this married entrepreneurial couple was, "it's not about what you make but more importantly, what you spend that counts." I was living life large and they could see the cliff coming for me well before I could. Walt and Monique's insight saved me more grief than I could have handled at that stage of my life, and they still have an important role in guiding me in my life and business some twenty years after first meeting them.

If you are young, the best thing you can do is find mentors and start learning from them. A properly mentored young professional should be dreaded by his or her competitors, as the energy they bring to the game, teamed with proper guidance, are a potent combination.

> ### Have a Major Drive to Succeed—A Plan—Be Detailing Smart
>
> When I opened my business detailing private jet aircrafts the people at the airport had bets on how quickly I would shut down. I had little money, we were located in a small market, others before me had failed, and I knew few people as I was in a new city and state. That was 1998. I did not let others' poisonous wishes beat me up or tear me down. I worked my plan, was dedicated, and open to learning from others. You will need to be the same if you are going to make it within any business.

As for you older crowd, don't think you can't be mentored just because you are older and wiser. You know better. Every old dog can learn new tricks, can't they?

Reality Check

I want you to learn the meaning of the word average: "of no exceptional quality or ability." If you perceive yourself as being average in life, then you will likely be average in business. If you are average, you gotta step it up and I don't want to hear, "Well, I am shy." Become un-shy. If you are looking to start a business you can't be shy, you can't be average, and you can't make excuses.

If shyness or lack of people skills are holding you back, you have a couple options: Expand your comfort zone and become that people person you have not been up until now, or move on to another business. A detailing business is a personality business and those who marry detailing abilities with business abilities are going to win wars. So, why not expand your comfort zone and start connecting with people at a new level? You may just like it!

A Look at What Detailing Is

Detailing can mean many different things to many different people depending on where you live and what your local market's economic climate is. In upper-middle class to high-end markets, your prospective client base will be familiar with detailing for the most part.

In middle income or lower end markets, detailing can mean a quick wash-and-wax job or, get this, some people within some markets think detailing is customizing cars for dealerships. They believe detailers provide pinstriping or provide add-on items—a far cry from what detailing really is.

Modern-day detailing is a combination of science, technique, proper products, and passion for what you do. Vehicles are more complex than ever and the days of being a champ at washing dear ol' Mom's car, then going out and starting a professional detailing company are GONE. If you treat your detailing business like a joke, you will be a joke.

Detailing has become a trade and detailing is a true art form when performed at the highest levels. It is a super-competitive business, and if you are going to play the detailing game, you better be ready to play the game right!

Our industry, as a whole, can be divided into three groups:

- The first is the "I don't care. I think I know it all, but in reality I know nothing about detailing correctly" group. This is the crowd that places value on "beating" everyone in town and offering the lowest price. The same group performs "destructive detailing" and while the work may look great, the results can be reached at a very high expense to the car, and the customer. Healthy clear coat is devoured as quickly as a great white shark can eat a foot-long hot dog, and healthy clear coat can not be recovered. When the paint system is compromised, there is no help for the poor detailer who details behind this group. But with some luck, that detailer is well equipped to recognize a possible situation by having paint gauges on hand. (The clear-coat level on a modern-day car is a clear or sometimes tinted protective layer applied during the painting process. It is designed to be a protective layer over the paint to help protect, enhance, and act as a sunscreen layer for the paint itself. This layer of "clear" is what we as detailers correct, polish, and protect.)
- The second is the "highest quality at any cost" group. Let me tell you, for two years I had "addicted to shine-itis" and when I looked at the numbers—the dollars and cents within my detailing business— I was shocked at how much my addiction to shine was costing me, and how much money I was giving away to the clients. I love to make a car as new as new can get just as much as anyone reading this. My passion for detailing is only trumped by my passion for cars, which is a double whammy. I love making paint and interiors sparkle but just a couple years into my business (a very long two years I may add), I jumped to an elite group within the detailing industry.

What I Wish I Had Known Before I Started My Business

Jason Rose

Global Technical Services & Training Manager: Professional Products Division

Meguiar's, Inc.

Support Structure

Thirty years after starting to detail cars, I think I know a lot now. I still learn new things about detailing and about the business every day, but I would say my knowledge level is high. In fact, I would say if I started a detailing business today I would have a high degree of confidence, know pretty much exactly what to do, and very likely achieve what I would perceive as an extremely successful detailing business. But thirty years of gathering knowledge and experience can lead you to that kind of confidence and assurance.

However, if you have not yet started a detailing business, never had any experience with it, and are just now looking into what it takes—even if you are a very self-confident person—how do you have the assurance that your business endeavor will be successful? In a start-up situation, what would it take for you to get up every morning, look in the mirror, and say to yourself, "You know, I don't have all the knowledge. I've never run a detail business before, but I feel pretty confident my business will be successful. And I'm excited about what I'm doing today." Wouldn't that be a good feeling to have as you start your new business?

Well, that is not how I felt starting my business. Truth be told, I was shaking in my boots. I felt scared and out of control. I loved polishing cars. I liked to make customers happy. I was digging the instant gratification of a transformed, shiny car and cash in my hands. But beyond that, I had no idea what I was doing. I was going day by day, car by car. I was in a gray area somewhere between "this thing is about to flourish" and, "wow, that was close" when a mistake, excessive bill, damaged car, dry spell, failed sales/ marketing campaign almost ran me in the ground!

But I have really good news for you! Today, a detailing business start-up doesn't have to be that way. Well, it didn't have to be that way for me in the 1980s either, but that's how I did it. The business environment is different now. And you have more resources available to you now than I had in 1982. Here is a partial list of the noteworthy:

1. Professional detailing associations.
2. Detailer support networks (with regularly scheduled conference calls and webinars).
3. Training classes, seminars, and workshops—both in detailing skills and detailing business expertise. (Do as many as you can afford. Do them frequently. Choose trainers carefully.)

4. Formal and informal mentoring: support/training/coaching from industry leaders and product manufacturers.
5. Good books, like the one in your hands.
6. Web-based detailing discussion forums. (Be careful with this one. The Internet is uncensored, as it should be, but don't make the mistake of assuming everything anyone writes in a chat box is factual, useful, or relevant to you.)

For the first five to six years of my business, I didn't do any of the above. Most of it didn't exist. And some of it was just beyond my reach. I didn't know how to connect with it. But now, you are a few clicks away from connecting to the "start buttons" on any of the above. And don't underestimate the power of engaging in a full support system around you. Today, it will make or break your business.

I really hope you get the volume and tonality of my message. I am not suggesting. I am not encouraging. I am not gently nudging. I am telling you emphatically and unequivocally: if you want a feeling of strong confidence and complete assurance that your start-up detailing business will, no doubt, be successful you need to be doing each and everything I have listed above. (Don't take my word for it, ask a successful experienced detailer today just how important these things are to a start-up detail business.)

Let Me Describe the Feeling Again

You get up every morning, look in the mirror, and say to yourself, "I don't have all the knowledge. I've never run a detail business before. But I feel pretty confident my business will be successful. And I'm excited about what I'm doing today."

If you want that feeling I'm saying you must be actively engaged in the above six support systems. Unfortunately, I have seen way too many detail businesses fail recently. And fortunately, I am connected with many very successful detailers all over the world. I have personally experienced and witnessed many things that work, and many things that don't work. Trust me on this one, you will not automatically be successful because you read this book. Hopefully, this book gets you thinking about things and guiding you into your next steps. But the formula for success in the detailing business today is in the six things listed above.

Notice I didn't say you need to be an expert detailer with strong detailing skills. Notice I didn't say you had to have a business degree or be a business expert. I have seen many excellent detailers fail in the detailing business. And I have also seen very proficient businesspeople fail as well. The key is a healthy balance of the two. General business expertise or knowledge is not sufficient. It's a good start, but what really matters is business knowledge specific to the detailing business, and you get that by "rubbing shoulders" with other detailers and mentors in the business.

The Right Tools

I'll leave you with a fun story about my detailing skills when I started my business. It's a little embarrassing for me, but here goes. (Is anyone I know reading this book? Ha-ha.)

In the 1980s, machine polishing paint was predominately done by rotary buffer. The massive Dual Action Polisher movement in the business today was in its infancy and most detailers didn't even know what a D.A. tool was (myself included). In general I was afraid of machine polishing, so the first few years of my business I got real good at hand rubbing out cars. I was young and full of energy, and only mildly fatigued much of the time. (If I had to do that today, I think I would drop dead with the applicator in my hand!) But I spied—I mean, happened to drive by and observe—other detailers using machines. So I was curious what that was all about. Should I do machine polishing?

I did two things that shaped my business for the next ten years:

1. **Shopped my competition.** Those are the current words to describe it, but all I knew at the time was that I wanted to learn the what and why of machine polishing from my competition. I didn't know where else to look. So I had my mom take me and her car to a variety of detailers in my area. She would ask about services offered and how the detailer intended to polish the paint. When the topic of machines came up, she would ask many questions about the tool, process, results, and risks. I stood there posing as a silent bystander just listening, quietly soaking it all in. They bagged on-hand application and said that machine polishing was the only thorough way to remove paint defects. Detailers polishing by hand, they said, "are doing so because they are not true professionals and don't know how to use machine polishers." Ouch. (I said to myself, of course.) So there you have it, I was shamed into my decision to use machine polishers. From that day forward, I wanted machine polishing. I was a professional, darn it! I say so, so therefore I am. Silly hand rubbing, that's for those other type of people, you know, the nonprofessionals. After all, I was just out of high school. It was time I grew up and did what the big boys did.

2. **Purchased supplies and equipment** from an ad. A detailer advertised in the paper that he was getting out of the business and had everything needed to start/run a mobile detail business, including three machine polishers. Five hundred bucks takes it all. It was several milk crates (seemed to be standard operating equipment for mobile guys at the time!) full of compounds,

polishes, waxes, and chemicals. Pressure washer. Vacuum. Generator. Water tank (which was a fifty-five-gallon plastic recycled drum). And three different polishers; a Gem ten-inch orbital, a Cyclo Dual Head D.A. polisher, and a Sioux rotary buffer. I felt I got a good deal. The guy gave me a quick five-minute demo of how each of the three machines worked. I gave him my five hundred bucks and I was on my way. But unknowingly at the time, in one purchase I had come across the three major categories of machine polishers, and had begun my lifelong fascination with machine polishing paint.

So with five minutes of instruction and demo on each tool, I now was in the machine polishing business. They appeared easy enough to use when the guy demonstrated them. How hard can it be?

Which one would I try first? The Gem orbital was big, bulky, and heavy. The Sioux rotary was loud and felt like a two-ton boat anchor! So I defaulted to the least intimidating which was the Cyclo D.A. polisher. All three were very used and very old.

My next three customers' cars represented my first experiences with machine polishers of any kind.

What follows is embarrassing, so put on your nonjudgmental hat and roll with it. (Not too many people know what I am about to share.)

NOTE: Do not do what I did. You should never experiment on a customer's car. If you are new to machine polishing, get properly trained by a qualified and reputable trainer. Then practice on hoods and body parts from the junk yard. Here's why:

First Car—the Cyclo tool looked strange. Two four-inch polishing heads with a right-angle handle and a hand grip on top. It was smooth running and didn't vibrate too much. I got the hang of it fairly quickly. It was removing defects better than I ever could by hand. I was getting excited about this machine polishing stuff! I nearly got the car done when I got paged (OK, I am dating myself with that statement). I set the tool down on the deck lid but when my hand left the tool handle, I inadvertently switched the tool on. It hopped and bounced and flew off the car! Seven hundred dollars for damages to the deck lid.

Second Car—the Gem was huge in my hands. It was a big round ten-inch, could have been eleven-inch pad with a heavy fat motor on top of it. This was a two-hander for sure. Free spinning in the air, it vibrated so much I thought it was gonna knock me over on the ground. But when I put it to paint it seemed smoother. The guy showed me how to put bonnets on this thing, so I did that carefully and proceeded to polish the car. I had not yet learned to switch the tool off before pulling the tool away from the paint, so when I did the bonnet shot like a rocket off the tool, bounced off the moon, and landed back on earth somewhere just out of my sight. In the same instant, I instinctively tried to stop the monster in my hands from gyrating my arms off by grabbing the pad with my left hand. (In hindsight, the switch might have been a better approach.) Somehow my thumb got sucked into the machine and I felt pain. I had many words in mind, but "ouch" is what came out. A five-hundred-dollar trip to the doctor for the shredded and bruised thumb. The doctor didn't do anything about the bruised ego however. The injury was far from serious, but I felt like an absolute goof.

Third Car—I was very cautious with the Sioux buffer. I had heard some nightmare rotary stories and the previous machine was unfriendly. It was hard to pick up for the first time. It felt unusually heavy for something you were supposed to use in your hands. But at least it didn't vibrate. And it didn't seem to have any place my thumb could get stuck in. It just required all of my arm strength to hold it upright. But I was a "professional" and fully intent on rising to the occasion. I had this beautiful nearly new Mercedes Benz to do with very minor paint defects. So I picked the mellowest buffing pad I had. I picked the lightest duty polish I had. I put the tool on the lowest speed setting. I was gonna wade into these waters slowly. As I started to polish, the tool had an incredible pull to one side. I started to wrestle with it, fighting to keep balance and control. Fortunately, it had a trigger switch so all I had to do was lift my finger and the wrestling match stopped. Wow, was that an awkward feeling. Really? Was the rotary supposed to feel this uncomfortable? I managed to apply the polish down the side of the car when I decided to stop (to give my arms a break) and wipe the polish residue off the panels. I remember the moment like it was yesterday. The image is burned in my psyche forever. I wiped off the residue on the fender to reveal strips of primer showing on the edges! There was beautiful metallic blue paint, with burned-through gray primer showing on the ridges and edges. With my heart not pumping and no air being exchanged in my lungs, I wiped off the remaining panels to reveal more of the same. I sat stunned on the ground for a second or an hour, can't recall which. A three-thousand-dollar charge from the paint shop and an angry, upset customer who never spoke to me again. (And this is how the Lord works. I didn't have the three thousand dollars, so I worked off the money part-time in the paint shop over the next four months, and, get this, I had to be assistant to the "master" painter/polisher. He wouldn't let me touch the rotary, so I did important stuff like wash/dry cars, move cars, hold his polish bottle, wipe polish residue, and get his coffee. You know, professional stuff. But I also got to watch someone rotary polish up close. Watch for many hours, I did.

So my first experiences with polishing machines were not very positive. What happened after that? It was five years before I ever put a rotary polisher to paint. I mastered the Cyclo Polisher. I studied, experimented, practiced, and completely understood that tool's capabilities, strengths, and risks (which were low). It evolved into not just my go-to machine polisher, but became the positioning and marketing message of my company. I was the "guaranteed no swirls" detailer in my town. I became the detailer with the reputation for getting the most challenging black cars machine-polished beautifully with "guaranteed no swirls every time." I also became known as the go-to guy for fixing swirl marks from other detailers' rotary work.

But here is the kicker, and my point to you: My marketing message of "guaranteed no swirls" was either brilliant or borderline deceitful. My customers didn't know that I was deathly afraid of the rotary. They didn't know I didn't know how to use one. They didn't know that it was not possible to leave swirls with a Cyclo tool. The borderline deception was that I allowed my customers to believe I was proficient with machine polishing. The fact was, I could not rotary polish cars. I didn't know how. So in that sense, the Cyclo approach felt like a crutch to me (at the time).

About halfway through the lifespan of my detailing business (about six years into it), I picked up a rotary buffer again. I went to training classes. I practiced on junk cars and family cars. I went to a Meguiar's clinic on rotary-polishing technique, and to learn about their new polishing system. I started to feel more confident and began using it on customer cars when needed.

Fast forward to today. I enjoy rotary buffing very much. My skills with a rotary have been so honed, that I feel I can buff cars with the best of them. I can walk up to any car in almost any paint condition and jump on it without any fear or hesitation whatsoever. The rotary, and D.A. tools for that matter, feel like extensions of my arm. I am so comfortable with them. I've buffed on multimillion-dollar cars. I've rotary buffed on award-winning show cars with paint jobs costing thousands of dollars. Heck, I've rotary buffed on Barry Meguiar's car. And currently, I train detailers, salespeople, and trainers around the world on rotary buffing techniques.

I am proud, but not bragging. I share my embarrassing beginning to machine polishing and my current high level skill set for a reason.

What I wish I would have known before I started my detailing business? I wish I would have mastered the rotary buffer sooner! My belief is that proficient detailers who want to be able to handle the broad variety of paint variables, customer requests/expectations, and have the confidence to handle any repairable paint defects need to master the rotary buffer and the Dual Action Polisher. In my opinion, both are necessary tools in the professional detailer's tool box. One without the other has limitations. D.A. polishing has become more powerful these days, with lots of advances in tools, polishing pads, and technologies. But, there are simply some things you will not be able to do if all you could do was either D.A. polish or rotary buff. I've always said that the best tool a detailer has is between the ears. Be smart. Step up. Seek out training. Master both major polishing machines; rotary and D.A. Polisher.

- The third and most elite group is the "pros turning a real profit." This group is about as rare in our industry as a truthful politician is in Washington, D.C., these days. Many detailing players are out there talking the talk but few have a checking account with assets that would prove any real success. The professionals making the most impact know and understand that profitable detailing involves building proper systems and processes, and that a growing detailing business evolves, changes, and adjusts to the ever-changing detailing world.

Which group do you belong in or desire to belong in? Being a fantastic detailer is not an option. To be profitable you must be a talented detailing technician in today's market. To survive, you must be detailing smart and be a business person first, a detailer second.

A Few Detailing Realities

Detailing is a physically demanding business. You need to enjoy working with your hands and be in condition to perform the work.

Detailing is a work of love. Those who are passionate about the automobile have a success rate far higher than those performing detailing simply for the money. If you are going after detailing for the money, put on the brakes and rethink this decision.

Do you enjoy your own detailing efforts on your car? I know of detailers who are, for a lack of a better word, pigs, and their success has been mediocre. The pros I know who are making the money, and have built a solid business, keep their own cars nice and clean. Some are even perfectionists.

Do you have an eye for a nicely detailed car? Some see paint, others see a canvas. The people who succeed can see imperfections. They may not know what they are, but they know they should not be there.

Perfection or profit? There is a nasty disease within detailing known as "addicted to shine-itis." I am all about the perfect detail or the perfect car being detailed perfectly, but so many within this industry fail due to this level of perfection. Perfection is OK, as long as the customer is paying for it. Can you separate perfection and profitability? The best can, and do!

Is the Timing Right to Start a Detailing Business?

As I write this book, the economy is in the tank, jobs and careers are insecure, and people are losing homes at the highest levels in modern times. With that said, there are fortunes being made. BMW and Mercedes-Benz are breaking sales and profit records and the used car market is hot. The messages we are reading are mixed, so let's talk about evaluating the scene.

- Many markets are flooded with detailers. You need to face reality and do some investigating within your market. In Southern California for instance, where my home is located, detailers are like cockroaches in many areas. So-called detailers are all over the place, and many fail to be on solid foundations so they struggle, and most fail rapidly. The people starting these businesses make the failed assumption that a detailing business is a piece of cake to start and their road to riches is paved with wax. Almost before they know it, they are out of capital, have damaged some vehicles by having no detailing education, and now their reputation is damaged. They start giving away their work by offering cheap prices and "beating out the other guys," thinking that it will get them more business and save their business. That is what usually helps them along to their demise and death as a business.

- That constant creation of new, then failing, businesses. This has damaged this industry nationwide. Why? When uneducated, undercapitalized businesses start up, most make one common mistake: they devalue their services and drive the price of detailing services down. This in turn plays havoc with legitimate detailing businesses. Then, with so many practically giving away detailing services, it makes it very hard for the legitimate detailing firms to make it. Or does it?

  When a market is crowded with other detailers, what could make it a good market to enter? Every shop I have ever started or fixed—mobile or home-based—was established within a market that already had competing detailers. Competition does not bother me and to be direct, competition encourages me to work hard. Here is what I look for within a market before I start the detailing business:

  1. **Booked-up Shops**—When I call around and detailing businesses are booked up more than ten days ahead or if they are two–three weeks out, I get very excited as I can come in and gain market share pretty quickly.

2. **Market Interest**—I am a car guy and if people are asking me where I get my car detailed, BINGO. I am going to research that market to no end.

3. **Weak Competition**—The economy is bad right now and some detailers are very unhealthy economically. If you are business savvy and have a fair amount of start-up capital, you can finish off the weak within your market and gain market share rapidly.

4. **Market with Money**—I don't care how many detailers there are in a market. If that market has a history of supporting disposable cash businesses like detailing and I am connected with the money people within the town, that is a good sign!

What I Wish I Had Known Before I Started My Business

Michael Pena
Mobile Auto Detail
Houston, TX

Certainly it is very simple to reflect on the past instead of looking into the future. One thing I wish I had known before I started my business is that passion and a desire to succeed will only take you so far. Passion for doing a job well done gets me out of bed every day. The desire to succeed takes me from job to job. However, beyond that one needs firsthand knowledge of basic principles. Even after all these years, there are still many questions I seek answers to such as:

How much time should I allow for an appointment?

How much staff do I need?

What is the best product for a particular situation?

Should I advertise in the newspaper?

Do I buy a building or rent?

I wish I had known more about developing my business. Maybe I should have enrolled in business classes. Back then I was searching for technical knowledge and how to perfect my results. Today, I am building my company's strengths and maximizing my weaknesses to turn them into assets.

I love to see detailing being done wrong. I am all over a market where no one is offering detailing done right.

Detailing Is an Easy to Start Business, Right?

I talk with all too many people who love this view of the detailing world: "I used to detail my own car" or "I detailed my parents' car and they loved it." Of course they did, you were their kid and you probably did the work for free, or for the right to the car keys on Saturday night. But free brings low expectations, even from good ol' Mom and Dad.

Detailing professionally for people you don't know, who also have high expectations for their purchase of a detailing service, is an entirely different world than detailing your car, the family car, or your friends' cars.

Casual, hobby-based detailing is what started my own passion, but I do think it's important to know that it takes a great deal more to make it at the professional level.

Here are a few additional misunderstood tidbits about detailing I would like to clarify:

- All I need are a few things from the local store to get started—Professional-grade detailing products are often not so easy to find in your local market. The corner auto-supply store is not going to give you the level of products you will need as a professional. (In the back of this book I have listed several of the most popular Web resources for gaining access to professional-grade products.)
- The $85 to $150 retail detail—Here is another key term I wanted you to burn into your head: "full detail." I hear this common and overused term all too often. The term "full detail" is dangerous and pricing that level of service within almost any market has one meaning, maybe two. In short, the first meaning of the term means "struggle." If you are going to offer a full service detail at the $85 to $150 mark, I can tell you now, you will struggle to make a true profit. Offer the service below that mark and the second meaning is "failure." You need to understand that your new venture is a business. You need to make sure you understand the pricing demands and related costs of running a business. If you price your services too low, it can destroy your business or, at a minimum, burn you out, and fast!
- The $1,000 detail—Performing a $1,000 detail seems to be a big goal for those new to detailing and I am not sure where this comes from. I know that many of us are car people, and that working on one-of-a-kind vehicles is very

attractive, but the reality is that this level of detailing is very uncommon. Do pro detailers perform at this level? You bet they do, but it takes years to build up that level of reputation, and that level of detail is rare even for the most elite-level detailer. Few are making a living solely from this level of service but I encourage you to set your goals high. I would rather shoot for the stars and hit the moon than fail because I didn't set my goals too high!

- All you need are two customers a day to make big bucks and really to succeed within detailing, right?—When I started, I made a massive error. I underestimated how hard it would be to attract new customers. Directly related to that error, I missed my first year's sales goals by a mile. That was many, many years ago and I now know that thinking I could find two new detailing customers a day, ten new customers a week, forty new customers a month or a total of 480 new customers in my first year was nuts. Yet, today there are many suppliers that preach basically that you can make big money detailing just two cars a day. What is missing from this nonsense is how you are going to find those 400-plus new customers that first year. It's simply not that easy and as we progress, you will see that if you market your business and services correctly, you don't need that many customers in the first place to run a successful business.

Detailer Tip

When you use the term "full detail," your customer reads that as being complete and all inclusive. So, if the customer has road paint on the outside of the car and dog hair in the interior, along with heavily stained carpets, they expect that you are going to cure every ailment their car has.

If you sell detailing services this way, be prepared to be broke and work yourself to death.

Build a smart detailing menu and take the time to educate your market.

NOTE: Loosely used, the term "full detail" is common within the detailing industry as a menu item. Be careful with this term as it tells your client that everything is included within this service. Including everything within any level of a detailing service is not a wise move for any detailer.

Procrastination Is a Thief in the Night

I talk all the time with people who love viewing the detailing world from the safety of their porch or from behind the keyboard of their computer. Analysis paralysis is real, and all too many people analyze the industry, the investment, and spend countless hours looking at online forums, blogs, and watching YouTube. Hours turn into days, then weeks and even years. Performing your due diligence is important and necessary, but at some point you need to make a move based on sound research, drive, and you guessed it, passion. Life goes by fast; make a move in one direction or the other. Idleness is such a waste of your time. What's the worst that can happen, you fail? I would rather take a chance and fail than sit safely on the porch. Failure is sometimes the best teacher, and failure is a much better option than living a stagnant life.

02 Envisioning Your Detailing Business

When I started my detailing business, it was never about the right logo, the right timing, or having everything I needed to succeed in place. My drive was first survival, doing something that I loved to do, and getting the word out that I was good at it. I knew I had to connect with my market and I had to steamroll my competitors, not with fancy marketing or bling, but with personality and skill. I had little capital and knew that my wife and I had to use our people skills and my detailing abilities to win people over.

Yes, I repeat, I had little capital, but I had ten times the drive I needed and I had three kids that needed food, a roof over their heads, and some comforts in life. Not only did I want to succeed, I had to succeed! I knew my detailing business had to have a low overhead and I had a small budget to work with for the start-up. Making sure I made the right equipment and products-purchasing decisions were hugely important.

I also knew I had weather to deal with during the winter months when profits would drop during fall, winter, and spring seasons. With the above in mind, I set out to build my personal and professional brand.

Why develop personal and professional branding for both you and your business? Being a small business is a badge of honor. Getting your name and business name out there is very, very important. You want to be known as your market's go-to detailer, the local expert of experts. Your personal name and brand are important, just as important as your business name and image. You are the business and people need to know it!

With the above said, there are many elements within your vision of a detailing business that you will need to pay attention to. Following are a few of the key elements I would suggest you take a good, solid look at.

Going Mobile or with a Fixed Location

Let's start out by giving you some basic terminology pointers for this section.

- Mobile Operation—This is where you build a system that can take your business to your customer's home, office, or remote location. A mobile system can consist of many options these days. You can use a small SUV, minivan, truck, cargo van, or trailer. The options for mobile detailing systems are incredible.

- Fixed Location—This is a warehouse, former gas station, or building where you place your detailing business and customers come to you. For some, a fixed location can be at home or in a garage, outbuilding, or barn. This is not ideal in all markets, but I know of several people who have a nice detailing studio right at home and this option certainly does save money and can offer a great quality of life. I will advise that if you are setting up at a residence, think about legal issues with homeowner associations, cities, and counties as all of these agencies have rules and regulations pertaining to home-based businesses. Another concern is perceived value and how your clients might view this. I once had a studio at my residence and for me, it worked out fine. It was a great situation, and one worth thinking about for your business.

I will share this with you: I am a strong believer in going mobile when you first start a detailing business. My reasons are cost, long-term debt, and how hard you are going to have to work when you first start. Debt is a killer within business, especially if you are already tight on start-up funds. The mobile detailing model is not only the ideal start-up system when you are getting your business off the ground, it also offers the advantage of being a home-based business. Even today, whenever I can I work from my home because it also allows me time with my wife, kids, and my dogs. So while I have a sexy studio all decked out, when I have my choice and am just doing paperwork, administrative work, and marketing, I work out of the house. Here are all the facts I can muster on the positives and negatives of a mobile operation and a fixed location:

A Close-Up View of Starting A Mobile-Based Business

Positives	Negatives
Affordable to start	Weather can play a big factor
Low overhead	Will need to store while not in use
Moving billboard	Investment in the vehicle
Very attractive to customers	Can only service a single customer at a time
No rent or lease needed	Water regulations in areas you may service could restrict business
No utility bills	
Can be sold as a premium-level service	
Much larger service area	
Money saved can be used to build your business faster	
Great lifestyle	

A Close-Up View of Starting A Fixed-Location Business

Positives	Negatives
Not as affected by weather	Ongoing monthly expenses
Controlled conditions for high quality	Ongoing utilities expenses
Constructive for volume-based operation	Tenant improvement expenses
Could provide more visibility	More upkeep and maintenance
No travel time to and from jobs, allows more time for detailing	Set hours that you have to be there, so not as lifestyle-based
No need for set up and break down, complete system in place	Higher insurance expenses
	Smaller service area
	Business must come to you
	May take larger staff
	Can be more interruptions in your workday

I will tell you, having a shop is very convenient. I love walking into my shop each morning and not having to set up my equipment. I have collected everything I could possibly need, and never being too cold or too hot while working sure is nice.

There are many factors to think about when you are evaluating the type of detailing business you will be starting. Look long and hard at your local market and think about some of the items outlined above during your decision-making process.

I have had up to six locations at once and if I were to do it all over again, I would start mobile, concentrate on the services with the highest prospects of sales and profits within my desired market, and keep the business small, specialized, and quality-based. We are talking lifestyle here and mobile offers the best chance of success when you first get going within this industry. Remember, you can always grow into having a fixed location when you have the client base and therefore the capital to support a shop.

Retail versus Wholesale Detailing

Some of you have been around detailing and know the terms and phrases. For those who don't, we have two primary segments within the detailing industry—retail and wholesale. You may be thinking about going after dealership work within your market or maybe you are strictly all about going after the better-paying, retail-level work. I want to encourage you to look at both when you first open up shop.

You are going to need cash flow when you start up and I couldn't care less where that cash flow comes from, as long as you can make a profit. Retail is highly preferred, as there are more profits per hour in retail-based services.

On the other hand, wholesale accounts can offer an infusion of cash flow into your business and while the profits may not be as desirable, you can always drop or scale back your wholesale accounts as you build up your retail sales.

Small and Specialized versus Large and Volume-Based

Many times I see people wanting to go big within detailing. Believe me, there is nothing wrong with big goals but going big is not always the best answer, nor does going big mean more profits. Society today seems to be addicted to the bigger-is-better

Happiness is positive cash flow.

—*Fred Adler*

A Look At Wholesale Opportunities

Positives	Negatives
Provides needed cash flow	Low hourly profits
You can build up these clients faster in the early days of your business	Will be working on some nasty vehicles (but it is good practice)
Could supply you with a free or discounted shop space	To handle the volume, you may need to hire staff
Ability to practice and get better at detailing	Dealerships are demanding
Can offer add-on services such as headlight restoration, paint chip, bumper scuff repair	Will need to push volume to make a profit
	Dealerships are slow paying for the most part
	Dealerships are not loyal and always looking for cheaper prices
	Some dealerships may require you to have a fixed location yet you have no contract or security that they will continue to use you or even pay you
	Retention of staff is difficult within the wholesale segment
	Burn-out is high for wholesale detailing companies

A Look At Retail Opportunities

Positives	Negatives
Much higher profits per hour	Takes longer to build a client base
Retail clients can be very loyal	Less cash flow in the early stages of your business
Larger opportunity for growth	To handle the volume, you may need to hire staff
Can build a very rewarding referral program in retail segment	If you are mobile, you could be traveling more and thus on the road more
The condition of the vehicles you are detailing can be better	
Happier, easier to please customers	
Back-door selling opportunity	
Very open to mobile and fixed-location services	
You can work solo until you build up your business and retail usually takes a smaller staff and less volume which is good	
Much more supportive of a lifestyle business	

way of thinking and detailers are at the heart of this line of thinking. I want to share with you my feelings about what I have seen in the detailing industry when looking at both the large- and small-business models.

Let's talk first about the small, home-based mobile business. This business has low overhead, a small staff, maybe even just the owner working solo, or maybe with a helper or two. This model can accommodate both a high-end market that takes aim at the upper levels of local society or a more moderate market where the daily drivers are a blend of more average-level vehicles such as Fords, Chevys, Toyotas, and such. This smaller, easier-to-manage model offers a far greater lifestyle versus the larger, volume-based model. If I were to go back in time, I would keep my business specialized and aimed at the niche-based, going after those within my market that were looking for quality-based services.

The flip side of a small, specialized detailing business is the large, volume-based shop. Before we discuss this option, I know people who run these shops and love it. But, I know few who have what I would consider a lifestyle that offers much outside of work. I have been in this position and built up a sizable clientele, and while it did a great deal for my ego, it hurt my lifestyle, my hobbies, and took away time with my wife, kids, family, and friends. It changed me as a person. I was always driven but when I was running a big detailing operation, I got angry. All I did was deal with staffing issues and work. It was a huge pain in the butt and I hated it.

Taking aim at building your business into a sizable organization is not a bad thing. Just realize that detailing is a hard business to take regionally or statewide, and very hard to take nationally. Detailing is a business based on relationships, connections, and trust. Many think of combining retail and wholesale opportunities into one company. Mixing a retail and wholesale detailing business means, to me, that you need to have two crews; a dealership crew performing the wholesale work for dealerships while the retail crews performs the high-end work. Mixing the two is not ideal as staff will often over-deliver on the wholesale side or under-deliver on the high-end retail side. Either is detailing gone bad.

A big, high-volume detailing business can bring in the money, it really can, but at what cost? If you don't mind working a ton of hours, six to seven days a week, and addressing issues with staff at every corner of your day, a big detailing business could be rewarding.

Hundreds of times a year I am asked one particular question more than any other: "If you had to do it over again, what would you do different?"

Ego drove me in the early days. I wanted to be the biggest, baddest detailer in the United States. I worked very hard and within just a few years of starting my business, I had locations in several states. The money was there, I had a sizable staff, I had fame as I was starting to get national and international attention, and I had reached my goal of being big and bad. But there was one huge, massive, uncontrollable problem—all I did was work, and I hated every minute of it. I had a very young and growing family and was rarely doing the things I loved to do with them. Also, the largest portion of my profits went to staff and overhead. I kept very little of the gross sales yet worked my fingers to the bone. I had given up my lifestyle for what the world views as success, and it sucked.

Here is what I am doing today, and this is what I coach, teach, and mentor others to do:

- Be very organized in your business and have a clear vision of who you are, and what you desire out of life and your business. Anyone can work pointlessly. The smartest, happiest, and brightest work and live with purpose.
- Specialize within a certain market. I like to "follow the money" within a market and offer the services that deliver the highest profit points. This might be a $99 express detail or a $400 stage II detail. You will need to research the market, find the services your market wants, then build the services that match market expectations with your own profit expectations. Not all detailers are created equal. Build your menu based on what your market wants and the profits you need!
- Ask yourself: Am I going to sell hot dogs or steaks? There is money in both but you can't sell a steak-level detail for the price of a hot dog and that is what the majority of the detailing industry does. It's a major reason why so many detailers struggle.
- Network with successful people. There is a great quote that I have in my office and read daily:

> Stupid people surround themselves with smart people. Smart people surround themselves with smart people who disagree with them.
> —*Aaron Sorkin*

- Enjoy life and when work is done, it's DONE. Make sure to have hobbies and enjoy them. For me, my kids are a huge part of my life so taking time to do things as a family is important to me.

- My wife is a central part of my business and day care did not raise our kids. She helped build my reputation and assisted me in the sales and management of the business. Together, we have had a great deal of fun raising our kids in the car culture that detailing can offer. We are a small mom-and-pop business, and proud of it.

Can You Make This Detailing Business Happen Within Your Market?

Many people approach and ask me what it takes to succeed within business, especially when times are as tough as they are now. The answer to that repeatedly asked

Detailer Tip

When thinking of your detailing business, think about the lifestyle you wish to have. Maybe you are in your thirties or forties, enjoy time with family, and spending time doing what you love to do. If you want a lifestyle-based business, building a volume-based detailing business is not going to match your lifestyle wishes.

Some of you reading this may be young, in your twenties and you have big ideas and bigger goals. You are young and this is a great time to work your butt off, so maybe starting out with a high-volume shop is the answer for you.

Those who have succeeded at the highest levels are quality-based detailers concentrating on better servicing fewer clients. As I write this I am approaching my forty-sixth birthday, and I am young enough to remember my twenties and thirties and how important it was to be the biggest and baddest detailer. If I may, that was stupid thinking. Concentrate on being the best and the most profitable and enjoy life. Those six-day workweeks were a waste and knowing what I know now and what I am sharing with you today could have provided me with many more five-day workweeks, which could have built many more memories doing fun stuff and working a tad less. Do as I am doing now, not as I did then!

question is not easy. The answer is actually a combination of several factors, which include education (not just college), life and business experience, personality, inner drive, needs, and passion.

But all of the above cannot do much if you fail to plan, take action, and be educated in the art and war of the detailing business. Passion drove me to detailing and education, keeping ahead on business, tactical/technical detailing, marketing, sales, and a host of other elements have kept me at the top. Average does not work within business. Period.

If you are a business professional, do not kid yourself. You are at war within business and competing not only with those within your industry, but also an army of daily needs and desires your current and prospective customers have for other types of products and services.

Creating niches within industries has never been more important than it is now. Following the rest of the herd in the detailing industry is the worst thing you could do. Be a leader within your local market, do things differently than any other shop. Stand apart from the everyday shop and make sure you STAND OUT.

Knowing the art of detailing is HUGE but even more important—once you take your passion from hobby to business—is being a solid businessman or -woman. Passion drove you to detailing, right? Now sound business practices and devotion to education can make you a prime example of detailing done right. Continue to read, research, and network, and don't forget the importance of finding the proper mentors to assist you with your goals. Starting a detailing business is not hard. Making a profit is much harder. Matching a profitable business with the lifestyle you desire will be the biggest challenge you face. Be ready by being educated and well versed within all angles of the detailing industry.

Will Detailing Support Your Income Needs?

Now this is a loaded question but I am going to try and walk you through it. I know people who are clearing $30,000 a year within detailing and happy as could be while others making $100,000 a year are barely surviving. Let's talk about the $30K crowd. If you are in a small, low-cost-of-living area and looking to have a seriously fun, lifestyle business, detailing is it, and I know dozens at that very point.

On the flip side, I know people who are in major markets such as Los Angeles or New York and $100K a year does not go far in those areas. Now, if you are single and making that kind of money, then there is something wrong with your financial

Detailing Services Man-hour Guideline

The prices below are my professional suggestion depending on your market's tolerances and your detailing abilities.

The Service	The Express Interior and Exterior	Stage I Interior and Exterior	Stage II Interior and Exterior	Stage III Exterior Only	Concours Exterior Only
Price Range	$69-$129	$150-$300	$300-$450	$400-$800	$1,500-$7,000
Man-Hours	1-2 Man-hours	2-4 Man-hours	3-8 Man-hours	4-10 Man-hours	10-150 Man-hours

Before you read too much into the above numbers, realize that the above ranges are based on a nationwide opinion. If you are in Boise, Idaho, or maybe Milford, Pennsylvania, your prices are not going to be at the level of those in New York City or San Francisco. Each market is unique and you need to do a great deal of homework to figure out both your pricing structure and profitability. In addition, the needed man-hours for the related services will change in each market and is also based on your detailing education, abilities, the equipment and product investment you have made, and the condition of the vehicles you service.

responsibilities. However, if you are supporting a family and your spouse stays home with the kids, then I can see where your finances would be tight.

It comes down to this: Detailing is a blue-collar industry where you can make a nice living matched with a comfortable lifestyle. It is a great business to build confidence and business know-how. Many times, I see detailing leading into other, bigger opportunities. It has happened to me and I have watched others succeed by remaining in the vehicle appearance industry but increasing their income and net worth with additional businesses or by selling their detailing business and moving to other business opportunities.

To Do It All Over Again

Jason Rose

Global Technical Services & Training Manager: Professional Products Division, Meguiar's, Inc.

First of all, I WOULD DO IT all over again if given the chance. All thirty years of it. It's been an incredible ride. And I've met some amazing people.

However, looking back, there are a few things that were less fun. Some trials and tribulations I coulda, woulda, shoulda gone around instead of through. Mistakes I've made that I hope others don't make.

Standards and expectations—I think I was five years into my twelve-year business before I realized that I had become a master at overkill. Every car I detailed had to be perfect with flawless paint. If someone hired me to do the interior, I would do some exterior work anyway at no charge. A customer thank-you note wasn't a postcard, it was a three-page letter. If I needed a polishing tool, I would buy the best. If I needed a towel, I would buy the best. My mobile rigs could win Best Paint in car shows, and probably Most Elaborate Detail Rig if there was such an award.

I had the work ethic thing down. I put in 120 percent on every job. I had the image thing down. I had the best equipment and the best-looking truck. I looked professional all the time. I did my thing with lots of bling bling.

What's wrong with this approach? Aren't you supposed to go the extra mile to please customers? Isn't having all the best equipment and looking professional a good thing? Well, there is nothing wrong with this approach if you are getting paid at that level. In the beginning, I wasn't. In my first few years of business I did some incredible detail work. I had extremely happy and loyal customers. But I was working way too hard for each dollar. Compared to other detailers at the time, I was convinced I generated the best detail results around. But did I have the biggest revenue? Was I the most profitable? Not by a long shot.

The fact was—and still is today—that the average consumer is not able to distinguish between 100 percent flawless, defect-free paint and 50 percent reduction in paint defects on their car. And many are stoked, sincerely excited, and beyond satisfied to see the look of their paint with an increase in darkness of color and more gloss! So why was I working so hard for a show-car finish, when most of the time, I was the only one who could recognize what that was? And by the way, the few complaints and gripes I got were from customers who grumbled that I took too long on their car (doing the show-car finish that they didn't ask for, weren't paying for, and couldn't identify as such).

Additional evidentiary support for my overkill practice was this currently annoying fact (that somehow was beyond comprehension during my earlier years in business) that a show-car finish on a daily driver stays looking like a show-car finish for what, maybe a couple weeks at most?!

Wow, so glad I spent seven hours making that paint look absolutely perfect, for $55, so next week Mrs. Soccer Mom with 3.5 kids and two dogs could roll the minivan through the truck-brush, scrubbing-bubbles $4-car-wash fund-raiser at the church. After all, it needed a good wash because last week's rain caused Mrs. Soccer Mom to drive across the baseball diamond to pick up kids and equipment on the soccer field. (You think I'm kidding? True story. I made a minivan look flawless, so it could be absolutely trashed the following week.)

I must be a slow learner because it only took me five years to figure out that my let's-make-cars-look-perfect-for-little-money-customer-satisfaction program was flawed. I was barely making ends meet.

So I adjusted my standards and expectations, made more profit, worked less hours, and all the while maintained happy and loyal customer relationships. If I had the chance to do it all over again, I would have made this adjustment earlier!

When you go to McDonalds, you have choices at different price points. But you don't get to order the Big Mac for the kid's burger price. It doesn't work that way. When you go to the Mercedes dealer, you can't buy the high-end model at the entry-level price. When you go to your dentist, you don't get two crowns and a bridge thrown in with the teeth cleaning you paid for. I am not saying you should not go for show-car finishes as a detailer. I hope you get to enjoy the pleasure of doing as many show-car finishes as you want. I'm suggesting that you get adequate payment for the level of service rendered. Get paid for what you do. Consumers love options. Give them a good, better, and best choice with different price points. The only time you should feel guilty for doing a less than perfect job, is if the customer is paying for what they perceive is perfection and you aren't delivering. Otherwise, give them every bit of what they are paying for. No more. No less. Everyone is happy.

Slow growth versus fast growth—If you are in college, a mobile detailing business is a wonderful way to support yourself. The low investment, low overhead, flexible hours, and fast-cash income made it perfect for me. I recall working less hours and having more residual income than my college friends. It was, rather thankfully, a very slow-growing business. The priority was school work. So having too many cars to detail or too much stress to manage was undesirable at the time.

But when the business went full time, I expected the doors to blow out, flood gates to open, schedule to book up, and wallet to get fat. So what did I do? Signed a three-year lease on a nice condo, bought a second car, traded up to that big-screen TV I always wanted, and went on a nice vacation. You know, all the stuff you can't really do while in college but really wanted to. I knew what I was making part time, so I multiplied that by two, and that was my business plan to full-time detailing. But I'm not stupid after all! I made a budget. Duh. I calculated my expenses based on full-time detailing income. And I went about spending at that level. Problem was, I had not yet achieved that income level. So, for someone as smart as me, it didn't take too long before I figured out my business plan was a bit flawed. You guessed it, the business volume just didn't double overnight going from part time to full time.

This was my first real-world experience with being faced with a need for a growth strategy (two words I have become intimate with since then. It's an action item for any product, system, campaign, or training initiative I've worked on). Business growth seldom happens on its own. The gravity of that situation needs a counterforce upon it.

So the first snafu in my now full-time detailing business was the expectation that more time in, equals growth. The second faux pas was not having a growth strategy.

How fast do you want to grow? I mean specifically, down to the dollars per month/week. And please don't assume that "as fast as possible" is a good plan for you. In college, I opted for slow growth, which was the right choice for me. It worked extremely well. Super-fast growth might be what you are looking for. And that's OK. But beware that it is possible that a detail business can grow too fast and get out of control, which leads to a premature failure in most cases. I've seen it happen too many times. So don't just jump into the auto-pilot ride thinking that "as fast as possible" will get you there in a controlled fashion automatically. Really think through your desired growth rate. Be realistic given your situation. And be deliberate about how fast you want to grow.

What is the desired scope of your business? I mean specifically, down to the number of detail rigs, type rigs, number of employees, size territory covered, etc. Where exactly do you want your business to be in one year, two years, five years, and ten years?

Any growth strategy is not complete without three very detailed components; (1) what do you want to accomplish?; and (2) how fast do you want to be there? When you have complete clarity with these two things, you can then begin to understand and work through the steps you need to get there on schedule. So (3), the final component to a growth strategy is an action plan. Don't ask me how I know, but some detailers do it the other way around, take growth steps without completely knowing exactly where they want to go and how fast they want to get there. Resources, investment, and capitalization are vital. I started my business with a hose, bucket, a few towels, and a can of paste wax (Meguiar's, of course). I would earn a few hundred bucks, then put some money back in the business by buying more supplies, equipment, and operating expenses. I also covered some college and living expenses. And for the most part, I operated my detailing business out of the trunk of a car for a couple years with not much more than the stuff I started with. But the cycle I was in—earn it, spend some, reinvest some, earn some more—didn't provide for rapid growth. And as I've mentioned, it worked great for me in the beginning. But as a full-time business, it was a painful way to grow.

Large-ticket items took a long time to purchase. The equipment, products, or supplies that could immediately boost productivity took a long time to acquire and implement. The old adage, "it takes money to make money" is so true. More so now than ever.

Starting the way I did is certainly possible nowadays. But it is getting increasingly more difficult to pull it off successfully. I hope nobody tries it. The detailing business now is not what it was in the 1980s and 1990s. Consumers are more educated about detailing and their paint, so you have to know what you are doing.

Local and federal government has jumped in the middle of detailing, so you need to be compliant with a list of regulations regarding water conservation, water contamination, chemical storage, chemical dispensing, chemical safety, labor laws (if you have employees), and chemical transportation (if you are mobile). The surfaces on cars are changing more radically and rapidly than ever before, so how you reconditioned a surface two years ago might be causing damage this year. And technology in detailing equipment, chemicals, polishes, tools, and buffing pads is progressing quickly by leaps and bounds, so your daily processes today could be outdated and slow compared to what you could be doing. It's a precarious thing in the detailing business today, to not know what you don't know. Not only could you be a whole lot less competitive, but you could be doing things unsafe for the car or for you and employees.

So, even though I started my business and ultimately grew it without many outside resources and very little capital investment, I'm here to tell you: Please don't try that today. It was a tough way to go twenty years ago. It's exponentially more difficult today. The recent economic recession cleaned house in the detailing industry. It wiped out many a detailer. I say, your chances of success are better with sufficient initial investment and ongoing operating capital to support your growth strategy. How much investment and operating capital? Well, that depends (re-read the previous two sections). The larger the scope of your desired business and the faster you want to grow, the more critical a sound financial start will be to the health of your long-term detailing business.

While We Are at It, Let's Blow Some Myths Out of the Water:

- If you are looking to clear $100K a year within year one or two, look to a different industry. It can and has been done within detailing but it takes an extreme investment of both time and start-up capital to achieve this level of success that soon.

- If you plan on having a full staff perform the actual work within your new detailing business as you manage the day-to-day sales, bookkeeping, and other business operations, think again. You are going to need to start this business by grass roots, learn the systems and processes, establish the business, and then over a period of two to four years, bring staff into the picture. Detailing is not a hands-off business, unless it's tied to a full-service car wash or other business that has a ready made foundation for your detailing services.

- If you want to become a millionaire directly from detailing then, my friend, you have a rude awaking coming. Professional detailing is a great platform or springboard into other opportunities, but the reality is that detailing is not a rich man's game. While I know people who have become financially secure from detailing, we are talking about long, twenty-plus-year careers to arrive at that point.

- You can't be profitable with just a one-man shop? Bull. I am living proof that you can make a small, one-man shop work. I will say this, you will need to plan your small, one-man detailing business carefully as it takes a great deal of forward thinking and early planning to accomplish this task. A specialized and niche one-man shop can do very well, but I am kind of misleading you.

Detailer Tip

Check out my Detailing Success website, www.detailingsuccess.com, for updates, blog posts, and training events. I make many posts on my website sharing ways you can become a better and a more profitable detailer! You can sign up for our free detailing newsletter and be alerted when new profit, technique, and time-saving ideas are shared with the detailing industry.

To make the most of a small shop, I would suggest bringing in one to two helpers during the busiest times to assist you with increasing volume, and to give you a break on performing the simple tasks with the day-to-day actions you will be performing as a pro-level detailer.

Be Prepared: Success Means Sacrifice

You need to ask yourself this question: Am I prepared to work the hardest I have ever worked? Are you?

I make the above statement about sacrifice for a very pointed and direct reason. I don't care if you are going at detailing part time or full time. Getting the business up, running, and, more importantly, profitable is going to take a huge amount of work and, in some cases, some very long days, nights, and weekends.

If you are going to build this business, you need to admit and commit to working like you may have never worked before. Owning any business is difficult. But detailing is a luxury-based service business and your new business competes with your prospective clients' available disposable cash reserves and it's not a walk in the park to arrive at success in detailing.

Part Time

I have worked with dozens of detailing entrepreneurs who started out part time. Many where close to retirement and wanted to start ahead of schedule at building their client base while still employed in their careers. Some work in careers that allow some freedoms and time off. Firefighters and police officers in many cases are prime candidates to become detailing entrepreneurs.

- Tight Budget—If you are squeezing every dime to start your business, keep your job or at least have a part-time job to help pay the bills. When I started my business, I was a part-time sales technician at a high-end tool and supply store two to three days a week. I hated that job, but it paid the bills and allowed me to invest more and more in the business without going into debt. Having that job also gave me the energy, motivation, and desire to work harder and smarter within my business and not having to worry about the money aspect of life reduced my stress. Listen, stress will kill a business and stress kills creative thinking, not to mention that stress can kill you. Stress is simply unhealthy and I advise you to stay clear of it at all costs.

- Off-Season Reality—In your first couple of years in business, you will experience slow periods. Don't be too proud to take a part-time job in off times. As I explained above about my first year's part-time job, I went looking for a job in the winter where I would be around people who would purchase detailing services. Likewise, my wife took a job where she would be in direct contact with prospective clients. We worked this angle very carefully and our plan worked very well. I was a ski instructor and my wife worked as a waitress at an exclusive fine-dining restaurant. The contacts we both made were a sizable chunk of the starting foundation of our business. So keep an open mind to opportunities during the off-season of detailing.

Timeline to Success

As a small business owner, I am asked, "How long were you in business before you made a profit?" My answer is a clear, factual, and not all that enlightening: "It doesn't happen overnight." Can I be more specific? No, it all depends on your ability and the market you are located within.

You will need to decide how fast you want to and can grow while still offering exceptional service. Then map out how you will perform that level of service and stick to the plan.

Think of the tortoise and the hare story. You could do a ton of wholesale or low-end work making very little profit on each job and be very busy or you can do high-quality work at a fair market price.

Maybe you won't be busy every day but you will have time to focus on marketing and having openings for those who desire your skill. You may make the same money per year doing either one of these plans, but only one of these plans leaves you room to grow both your business and your lifestyle. Remember, detailing is a lifestyle business that given time and built correctly will offer you both an income and a life you can be proud of. You can build it fast if you like but beware that a fast-paced build-up could also burn you out. The more organized and well planned out your business is, the faster you can experience success.

Full Time

If you are going into the prime season of detailing in your market, you're educated within detailing (meaning you know what you are doing), and your detailing business is outfitted with the correct equipment supplies and cash reserve for sustaining you while you get started, congratulations! You are among a small group entering the detailing industry. Cash flow is always a real issue within any new business, so if you have the cash reserves to start, perform the proper start-up marketing, and keep your bills paid, go for it! The full-time option is usually the fast track to success!

Be Patient: Like Rome, a Detailing Business Isn't Built in a Day

Jim Goguen is a close friend and a professional detailing entrepreneur, and between the both of us we have over fifty years of detailing success. We are both firm believers that many entering the world of entrepreneurship fail to have the patience they will need to make it. Detailing success does not happen quickly and achieving your goal could take years.

A business plan is not an option but a must within your business. Most small businesses fail to establish any written plan at all, while others develop very in-depth business plans. I have found over the years to keep my plans directed at the fundamentals that will affect my business most. Within my plan, I include:

- A Feasibility Study/Outline—You can perform your own feasibility study, but if you are not sure of how to do this, it may be wise to purchase a study, but know that a solid feasibility study is not cheap. Do an Internet search for the term "how to perform a feasibility study" and you will find several guides on how to perform your own.
- Business Plan Outline—An outline of the business that includes the points covered in this chapter.

Strong Points of this Venture

What will assist you at being successful? What do you have above the others that really counts? Here are *some* points that display strengths. Be passionate, direct, and honest with yourself in this section!

1. Your Education—Degree in business
2. Your Experience—Accomplishments within your previous work and or business
3. Passion—A love affair with cars
4. Need—A need to succeed
5. Finances—Financial strength in the form of capital for this business
6. Experience—Will be trained and certified within detailing before the launch or you are already trained

Weak Points of this Venture

What are your weak spots within the business? Here are *some* points that display weak points. Remember to also be passionate, direct, and honest with yourself within this section as well.

1. Your Lack of a Formal Education—Do you know and understand business, marketing, and proper sales?
2. Your Lack of Experience—Lack of real-world business experience could be a real issue.
3. Lack of Money—Do you have enough funds to start and succeed?
4. Lack of Experience—Do you know professional detailing better than anyone in your market or can you learn it in a short time through training?
5. Competition—There are several detailers in your local area that may be more connected, better funded, and know more about detailing.
6. Weak Spots—Identify other weak spots that could cause issues within your business by using the "Addressing the Weak Points of this Venture" worksheet on page 46 to write down your key areas that need improvement.

Business Plan Outline

A business plan is a road map, a GPS if you will, for your business. If you were taking a cross-country trip to a state and city you had never traveled to before, would you leave home without a map or GPS? No, of course not, as this could be disastrous. Developing a business plan allows you to think ahead, plan, and address many items you may not have thought about otherwise.

If you are bringing on a partner, looking for financing, or trying to convince a spouse that your business idea has merit, a business plan is a must-have item. Speaking of partnering, a business plan is a great place to outline each partner's responsibilities, duties, and ownership within the venture. I would never partner up with anyone on anything without a well-laid-out business plan.

I use my own business plans as a calendar for outlining what I am to do within certain weeks of the year and within areas of the business such as marketing, sales, promotions, and events. This also allows me to plug in the cost of such actions, and provides a great foundation for planning my needs for capital.

Many think a business plan is complicated to build but in reality, a business plan can be pretty easy to construct. I am telling you, you will see strengths and

Addressing the Weak Points of This Venture

Weak Point

Solution

_____   _____
_____   _____
_____   _____
_____   _____
_____   _____
_____   _____
_____   _____
_____   _____
_____   _____
_____   _____
_____   _____
_____   _____
_____   _____
_____   _____
_____   _____
_____   _____

Now go line item by line item and address how you are going to deal with each weak point. Be direct and very, very calculated within this section!

weaknesses you would have never identified without performing the task. So go build your business's roadmap to success and for you guys that already have a business, that is no excuse, I promise if you utilize a business plan the right way, you will kiss me the next time we meet up.

A Blue-Collar Business Plan

This plan is what I dub the "blue-collar" plan, with no fancy charts and no attorney or accountant language. The plan outline above is a business plan that you can do yourself with a little homework. Also, note that a good business plan grows and changes and I suggest that you look at this plan weekly and make adjustments and notes. Make sure to follow the plan and make adjustments as you start to get a feeling for your business. The nice thing about this simple business plan is the fact that it's fast to adjust and make changes within. I like a plan with the flexibility that allows me to adjust and change on the fly as my business grows.

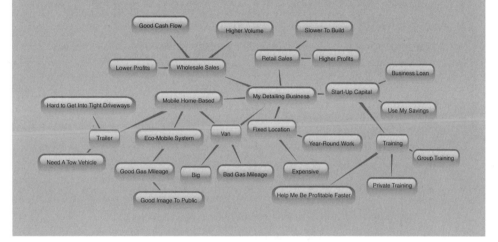

Marketing Plan

To gain access to your area's detailing customer base, these are the actions, steps, and resources we will utilize. Be very, very descriptive within this area and include the related cost for each of the items broken down by the week, month, and year.

Web-Based Marketing
This will include:

A. Website—Designed and built with this local market in mind

B. Social Marketing

C. Co-Marketing

Sales System

Once you do the above marketing, how will you sell your services? Do you know what sells, to who, where, what, and how? What is your call to action? What are your key points? Do you have a proper services menu? Explain your sales systems and the whos and hows.

Position

Describe your position in the market. How will you carve out your niche if the market is saturated, or how you will lead the competition if the market is small but competitive? For example, you might write: Our position within the local market is strong due to the fact that so few detailers are present within the market. Our detailing education, certification, and business knowledge, along with our level of connections within the local market will allow us to be the market leader within all desired levels of service we will provide.

Competition

In this section focus on outlining your direct competition and how you plan to exceed them in the marketplace. For example you may include: As part of our dedication to succeed this next year, we performed an in-depth review of each detailer within the area that we could locate. Here are our findings:

1. **Ed's Detailing**—In business for ten years, with a well-known name but a poor reputation. We found the company to be poorly managed with an absentee owner. We can provide better service, with better results, and be slightly above their price point, as our services and quality will be at far higher levels.
2. **Best Detailing**—Of the detailers within the area, this is the newest detailing company that is both mobile and fixed, with an outstanding reputation for high-end service and prices to reflect that quality. We are taking aim at this organization with quicker response time and fewer days to wait for an appointment.

Strategic Plans to Capture New Customers

Now that you have laid out the particulars about the competition, how are you going to earn and win over their customers in addition to new customers in the market?

How are you going to maintain those customers? How are you going to deal with slow-down periods? What is going to make you successful? This is the section that answers these questions. Review the following six points and explain each in detail.

1. Outstanding Quality
2. Outstanding Customer Service
3. Great Branding
4. Appreciation Marketing
5. Offline and Online Marketing
6. Become the Local Expert within the Industry

Operating Procedures

Within this section, explain who will do what and how in your company. See the following examples below and how they might be answered.

1. **Marketing**—I am going to incorporate the "Detailing Success Micro-Marketing" into my business.
2. **Sales and phones**—I have a smartphone that will assist me in managing my business with wireless ear pieces. This technology will allow me to detail and talk on the phone.
3. **Equipment upkeep and maintenance**—I will be performing daily care with repairs performed by an outside source.

With each area of your business, answer each and every item you can think of and this will keep the guesswork to a minimum.

Our Proposed Menu of Services

Describe the services you plan to offer. For example you might include the following:

Express Detail—Explain this service

Deluxe Detail—Explain this service

Signature Detail—Explain this service

Concours Level Detail—Explain this service

See our menu design e-book for more information—www.detailingsuccess.com

Proposed Sales and Profit Within Our Services Menu

Here is where you will explain your menu and the profits within each service. For example:

Deluxe Detail—$179 to $229 and, on average, will produce a gross profit of $40 per man-hour.

Extend each of your services out this way and track your profits per man-hour on each menu item.

Projected Sales Goals

I suggest you take this to a very in-depth level, down to the week, and make a fifty-two week goal sheet. This allows you to micromanage your business.

Weekly Performance Goal—$

Week One—$

Week Two—$

Hourly Performance Goal—Based on the above

Our goal is $ per hour within each hour we work.

Break-Even Analysis

To figure out your break-even analysis, take your cost out of your services along with taxes, and then figure out what it's going to take to pay back your investment. For example:

Total Investment Recovery—Here I calculate my earnings on my KNOWN man-hour performance. Notice I said KNOWN. So, let's say I am selling two, $200 details each business day. That is $400 in sales each day. Now let's assume you are selling that each day, five days a week, which equals $2,000 in weekly sales.

From my own shop experiences, I can perform my $200 detail in three to four hours. I am rounding up and going to say four hours per detail plus my travel time and prep time, so I am going to level this at a fifty-hour workweek. The product cost will be about $10 for each detail I perform at that level. So, for the week, my product cost will be about $100 for the basic products.

I then add in fixed cost such as my insurance, which costs me about $50 a week. I add in fuel, toweling costs, and then pad costs along with marketing, sales, and other random expenses. I do this by adding in another $25 per detail in "cost."

- Now we are at a total fixed cost of $400 per week for the bare minimum within your business per week. (Of course, your cost may differ.)
- My total sales for the week were $2,000, minus the above $400, which makes for a net of $1,600 before taxes, or $32 per hour net before taxes.

Some of you may be excited about making $32 an hour while others may be saying that is not all that much. If you could average that level of work year-round for, let's say forty-eight weeks out of the year, you would make $76,800 before you add in additional expenses and taxes.

You know the best thing about the numbers above? I had a $10-to-$12-an-hour staff member performing the work and cleared about $20 an hour on that one staff member day in and day out!

For my own detailing efforts when I am performing work on the collector cars and aircraft I specialize in, that hourly rate can grow to $85 to $200 per hour!

Personnel Within the Business

In this section, you will account for everyone involved in your business from yourself, to employees, to outside help. For example, you might include the following: In the beginning, I will be the sole staff member that will perform all duties within the business. I will outsource items such as:

- Bookkeeping
- Tax services
- Additional outsourced services—Within my shops, I outsourced some of the profit center services we offer like PDR (Paintless Dent Repair) and interior repair services. This allowed me to offer these services while having another business do the work for me, all while making a profit. They would charge me a discounted rate on their services and I would upmark that service, making a profit from someone else's efforts. Not a bad deal, is it?

Once the company reaches a level of certain dollar amount per day for a specified period of time, this will be the switch that triggers me to hire a part-time assistant.

- Sales at a level of (this amount of money) per day sustained for a period of four consecutive weeks, I will hire a part-time staff member.
- When sales reach (this amount of money), I will hire the staff member to go full time.

Capital Equipment and Supply List

If you are a new business, list all items that will need to be purchased. If you are an existing company, make sure you include the items/purchases you desire/need to make a complete makeover to your business over the next year. Make this a wish list and set these desired purchases up with goals. When you reach a goal, make a purchase based on sound financial balance but also as a reward for you and your business.

1. **Start-up equipment**—amount
   A. Trailer—amount
   B. Paint gauge—amount
3. **Training**—amount
4. **Business marketing goods**—amount

Keep adding to this list with dollar amounts.

Yearly, Monthly, and Weekly Capital Needs

Here is where you will lay out your business expenses, and make sure to make a budget per your local detailing season(s). Included within this area are items such as:

- Labor
- Taxes
- Rent/Lease
- Supplies
- Insurance

Take the above, and make sure that you know your daily, weekly, and monthly budgets. Again, micromanage your budget, and take it all the way to your hourly income projections. Your expenses will map out where you need to be hourly performance wise.

Assumptions Upon Which Projections Were Based

This section is where you will provide the reader of your business plan the specifics on how you arrived at your conclusions. For example you might write: This plan is based on research conducted and learned from our comparative shopping and research performed within an initial and ongoing feasibility study. Within this study we looked at various factors within the market such as age, trends, demographics, and other important factors relative to the automotive care industry within the local market. Here is a list of the information sources:

1. **Data website**—Name your source here
2. **Data source**—Name here

Be sure to include where all of your data came from, noting the website, book, article, author, etc.

Exit Strategy

Each business should know how it will be started but also how it will be ended. What is your goal, describe it here. For example, is your goal to:

1. Build your business up and sell the business in a given time frame?
2. Have a part-time business to provide you supplemental income?
3. Build a legacy business and turn it over for family/children to run?

To Do It All Over Again

Matthew Gillican
Advanced Detailing Specialists
Rochester, MI

Advanced Detailing Specialists has been in business for eleven years. We have had some ups and downs, but what business hasn't these days? I went to an auto-detailing school right away to learn the proper techniques, but I have never stopped learning. I have always tried to better myself as a detailer. Once you make a good name for yourself, word does get around. I started as a mobile business, which I think is a great way to start because you don't have a lot of overhead.

It is not easy. I thought it would be easy at first because when people found out I started an auto detailing business, they wanted to get their vehicles done. That kept me busy for a while. However, when those went away, I really had to go out and find business which wasn't easy since I didn't have any previous sales/business experience.

Writing a business/marketing plan is a must. I never wrote a business or marketing plan, so I had no direction at first with the business which was a big mistake! Doing a business plan shows who you are as a business and gives you a plan on where to go with it. A marketing plan does that as well. It helps you market your business and set sales projections.

Know what works for you and doesn't work for you, so that you can make the proper adjustments. Build systems into business. Have a complete system to detail a vehicle, so employees can follow that system to the letter. I know the system of how to detail in my head, but I never wrote it down.

Also, have a system for sales/marketing. This would be part of your marketing plan, but have a lot more detailed information. It would show what works to drive the business. You cannot be the only one to bring in business. It helps to have one or more people to do sales, so your business can run on its own without you having to be there every day. Everything from detailing, sales, customer service, money management, and leadership needs to be addressed.

Special Notes on Your Business Plan

In my early days of business, I was hard-core on my business plan design. I had everything laid out and every possible angle covered. By comparison my business plans today are sweet, direct, and very pointed to the profitability of my business and the lifestyle I desire to live.

I keep my business plan real, with no BS and no drawn-out, boring, never-to-be-read-again jibber jabber. My first plan for one of my current businesses was nearly one hundred pages long.

Today, that same plan for that same business is ten pages total and this plan has helped me more in recent years than my first plan ever could. You can get too involved and waste all too much time on a drawn-out plan.

I have had some incredible mentors in my life. One of my primary mentors, Walt, who I mentioned earlier, was the first to get me hooked on the phrase "It's not always about what you make, but what you spend!" I know detailers who make solid money, I mean a nice living. They live within their means and put money aside each and every week of the year. A few of these guys are

Ten Common Mistakes That Can Kill A Detailing Business

Like any industry, there are commonalities within detailing and I see ten common factors that play a part in the failure of many detailing businesses in their very early stage:

1. Failure to have the correct business education and/or business experience.
2. Failure to know how to detail at a professional level.
3. Business is underfunded and lacks any support capital to help them.
4. Starting out in debt or running up debt letting overhead get out of control.
5. Failure to have a written business plan addressing successes and challenges alike.
6. Failure to maintain sales pipeline and thus upsetting cash flow.
7. Failure to establish personal and business brand both online and offline.
8. Failure to establish an effective referral program.
9. Failure to be effective on the phone and poor people skills.
10. Utilizing a poorly designed menu and failing to make any notable hourly profits.

young—thirties and forties—and they have a very sizable nest egg of cash, invest-
ments, and retirement set aside.

On the flip side, I know people within the detailing industry who make over six
figures and have absolutely nothing to show for it. They live big, drive big, and talk big
but are in debt up to their eyeballs. "It's not always about what you make, but what
you spend!" Spend your hard-earned money where it counts most, and do as I have
done my entire life, find great mentors!

The reason I mention the common mistakes and success traits within this chapter covering your financial foundation, is that all of the items in both the positive
and negative columns need to be planned for. You need to think about the financial
demands of these items.

Spend Capital Where It Counts

You are excited about your new business and a detailing business to a car guy or
gal is like a toy store to a kid. All too many times, detailing professionals spend way

too much capital on items they simply do not need. We detailers are famous for also spending small fortunes on equipment and products, and many times we waste too much money on them.

Also, the amount of money people waste on marketing within this industry is insane. Most of the time, this money is spent on what I call panic-based marketing. Things slow down, people entering the detailing industry panic, and they start taking ads out within useless forms of advertising. Weeks later, business usually has not changed much, they are still slow, and the bills for the ads arrive, and that is usually when trouble starts. I am going to delve deeply into the marketing aspect of detailing later in the book, and I want to encourage you to really pay attention to that chapter. Doing so will keep you from panic-based marketing errors.

Building a Budget for Your Detailing Business Start-Up or Expansion

If you are just getting into detailing or maybe you are expanding and desire to take your detailing business to the next level, no matter if you are a veteran to detailing or brand new, you need to budget every aspect of your business. You need to know what ALL of your various costs are going to be, including your ongoing expenses. There are a few steps to follow to gain a clear picture of your overall costs and create a workable budget. First begin by building a start-up or expansion budget. See the "Example Start-Up/Expansion Cost" worksheet below for reference. Next, build an ongoing expense budget. See the "Example Monthly Bill Log" worksheet on page 60 for reference. Finally, build a wish list budget for the future. See the "Example Wish List Budget" worksheet on page 61 for reference. Following these steps will help guide you in the right direction for building a budget that will work for you and your detailing business.

Example Start-Up/Expansion Cost

I list every single investment I am going to make into this business. You are going to run into start-up cost that you have NOT planned for, so plan for them. Add in at least an additional 10 percent to that total number for the things you failed to plan for. There will be surprises, so list everything!

Expense	Cost	Priority (Y/N)
Incorporate	$349	Very early priority
Training and Certification	$2,900–$4,500	Very early priority
Mobile System (self build)	$5,800–$10,000 with equipment	Week four priority (following training)
Product Order	$1,700	Week three
New Domain Name	$9.99	Buy now
New Website	$500	ASAP, when I have cash!
Logo Design	$375	Now!
Marketing Kit (cards and hard menu)	$500	Week one or two
Opening Marketing Goods	$275	Week three

Over the years, I have learned that I need to see my bills and look at them a couple times a week, so I can calculate what needs to be paid and what needs to come in the door to pay the bills. There are times when this causes me to really hustle and make certain the bills are paid on time. Late fees will kill you! In addition, your expenses will assist you at making sure your menu will support your business. We will jump into designing your menu and profits later in the book.

Expense	Total	Due Date
House Mortgage	$1,349	1st of each month
Shop Lease	$1,200	5th of each month
Electric and Gas Bills	Averages $200 a month	15th of each month
Product Re-Order	Averages $225 a month	20th of each month
Domain Charge (for website)	$13.99	22nd of each month
Car Payment	$375.50	24th of the month
Insurance (car and business)	$375	24th of the month
Health Insurance	$475	26th of the month
Credit and Gas Cards	$475 (for all)	27th of the month

I have a constant wish list that highlights all the tools, products, marketing, and toys I would like to purchase for my business. I have those items associated with goals within my business and life. Here is how my wish list looks:

Item Name	Cost	Associated Goal
Join Big Bear Chamber	$249	Hit $2,000 in savings
Paint Gauge	$700	My first $2,000 week
New Uniform Shirts	$600	First $1,000 week
New Backup Polisher	$310	Hit $3,000 in savings
Test XYZ Paint Sealer	$125	By May 1st
Sanding Kit	$150	By April 1
Take Part in November Event	$800 (with travel)	Hit $4,000 in savings
Build Website	$500	First $1,500 week
New Wrap for Van	$600	First $2,500 week

So many concentrate on the possible income of a business, yet fail to understand the cost and expenses associated with the business. Getting a solid grip on your expenses will assist you at profiting within your business, believe it or not. Not knowing your expenses is a deadly sin within any business.

Shop Your Local Market and Evaluate Your Competition

When you go to the doctor for a check-up or if you are having a health-related issue, 99.9 percent of the doctors you visit will take your vitals: blood pressure, heart rate, and pulse.

Your vitals give your doctor a quick look at your general health. Shopping your market is a good way to judge the vitals of your local market and will allow you to get face to face with your competitor. To get you started on checking the vitals of your local markets, use the worksheet on page 63 for reference. This is what I look for in my market.

In my comparative shopping of competing detailers, I look hard at their level of connection within the community and also ask if local car dealerships, repair shops, or body shops are excited about my business. If your area is saturated with detailers, the car guys will usually be a good indicator of the health of your market. But I don't rely on that information alone, I dig deeper and so should you.

Questions	Yes/No/Good/Bad
Does my market seem economically healthy?	
Are other service businesses succeeding?	
Are my competitors good at phone sales?	
Are my competitors well connected within the market?	
Will the prices my competitors charge for their services support my business?	
Are my competitors capable and skilled?	
How is the presentation of my competition?	
Will my area better support a fixed location or a mobile service? Are other mobile businesses such as landscapers, carpet cleaners, and window cleaners doing well here?	
Who is the local expert and can I dethrone him/her?	
Can I increase the average price of a detail?	
Do auto industry people in my market seem excited that I am starting this new venture?	

Clearly Hear Your Market: It's Talking to You

The problem with most of us entrepreneurs is that we are usually pretty talented salespeople and we can sell ourselves on anything.

Don't sell yourself, convince yourself! I am not afraid of competition; I am not afraid of other detailers in the same market. All those items I can control, as I am very sure of my abilities as both a businessman and a detailer.

What I fear in a market is a lack of need, a lack of disposable income, cheap, give-it-away prices, and a market hooked on cheap prices for what they consider a detail.

On the flip side, when I travel around the country, I witness markets ripe for a true pro-level detailer like you. What pops out and tells me that the market is ripe?

- A bunch of nice cars that look like crap. Look around. Are there nice cars around town with raunchy looking paint? That's a market telling you that it may fall in love with you.
- I look at other detail shops and ask around about who is doing business with these shops and what they have to say about those shops. Are the shops well connected and respected?
- How are the local dealerships that sell higher-end models doing? This can be the highest levels of minivans or the local BMW dealership. High end is not just imports, but also domestic brands.
- How are other service businesses doing? I look at the local house cleaners, lawn services, and carpet cleaners. Markets that have successful service companies are always a plus for a market.
- Do you have large companies based in your area? Large corporations use many subcontractors which can mean a great opportunity for the smart detailer.
- A car culture or area that is car crazy is always a great sign. I live in a small town, but our town is car crazy and I stay pretty darn busy.
- Not a single detailer in your area aside from the local car wash? To all my car wash buddies, cover your ears for a second. Car washes are typically bad detailers. If car washes performing details are all you have in your market, buddy, you have a SERIOUS opportunity!

What message is your market sending to you?

What I Wish I Had Known Before I Started My Business

Rick Goldstein

RAGGTOPP Products

Atlanta, GA

Of all the qualities that go into making a detailing business successful, leadership is an essential ingredient. If you've got it, you know, and if you don't everyone knows.

I don't think you can be a great leader until you know how to give and take orders. Leadership is having the courage to ask questions no matter if you think they are petty or unimportant. It's always good to ask where a land mine is before you potentially step on one and cost yourself time and money. It costs you nothing to ask a question, and you will get an educated answer that will help you, your customer, and your business. Learn from your mistakes and move on.

The most creative and productive ideas will always come from individuals closest to our customers. You start a business not for the money, but for the freedom to be your own person. Turning your idea into becoming a professional detailer personally rewards you the opportunity to freedom. Having freedom allows you to think out of the box and offer the best product and services for your people and customers. Before you start down the path to becoming a professional detailer, be sure that you are not motivated by greed.

In retrospect, I had an idea about having a fabric protectant that would protect against stains and some forms of mildew and contain UV blockers. I was naive and thought once people see it, they will buy it. My friends told me I had a great idea. Yes, I had somewhat of a marketing plan, but never knew the importance of what stood between my product and the customer. No one told me, nor did I ask, why one product in a thousand makes it from concept to market. I quickly started writing down all my questions and getting the answers. Asking questions costs you nothing and you get back great advice and information.

Test, test, and test your products and services with customers, not your friends. Go out and ask twenty people who are not your friends or relatives what they think of your new products or services.

Simple questions and getting the right answers, not the ones you want to hear, is the most important.

What would you be willing to pay? (Insist on a specific price.) How many times a year would you use my services? Who are you using now and are you happy with their present service?

If you do not get the WOW factor to most of your questions, keep your life savings—and your current job—and move on.

Rule One: You can't be a great leader until you have been led.

Rule Two: Don't try to launch a new business or idea until you've tested the water. Test. Test. Test.

Run Realistic Sales and Profit Projections

There are profits to be made within detailing, but you need to address some real-world issues before those profits start rolling in. Here are some cold, hard facts to think about to help you build a solid detailing foundation:

- Can you perform at the same level with twenty-year veterans of detailing? Hopefully 98 percent of you are answering no if you are smart. It doesn't matter that you have detailed a few cars before. Once you go pro everything changes. This game is for money and you are competing with me. Will your quality match mine? It needs to right from the start. I could be your competition and you need to be able to handle me. Can you? Of course you can, but it's going to take you making a commitment. You are going to need to gain experience somehow. It might be working for another detailer or dealership for a couple of years. Maybe you train with a seasoned professional and take the fast lane to detailing success. No matter if you take your time and learn on the job, or work with a detailing coach, you need to know what you are doing. I get people in my coaching program all the time who started their business one, five, or ten years ago hoping to learn as they earn and all they have done is struggle. Having a detailing mentor or coach can cut years off your learning curve and help you realize real success much, much faster.
- You are going to be slow. When you first get going, you are going to need to practice, get your systems and processes in check, and you are going to be a tad on overload. And the fact that you will be trying to overimpress every single client you come in contact with means that the opening weeks of your business are going to be less profitable than you think. I tell people to start with a soft opening. For the first ten to twenty cars, do your parents', friends,' family members', and coworkers' cars. This will give you chance to get in a groove before you officially start your business with paying (and highly demanding) customers.
- You may not be properly equipped. You are going to need the best equipment, the best products, the best processes, and the best systems. Realize now that being outfitted correctly means one thing to your business: higher profits.
- Don't overshoot the projections, no matter what you read on websites and detailing forums. We could talk demographics here that include drive-by

counts for your location and the number of details performed per capita. But if you want to hear the truth, few have spent the money to do a true detailing study.

- Now with that said, there are studies out there, but they are combined with the car-wash industry and that affects the overall numbers drastically. Add in that our economy is in a downturn, and that confuses any demographics that have been established. When I review a market, I go to grass-roots investigations I outlined in the previous section on shopping your local market.

But if you want some numbers or percentages, I am going to share what my experiences tell me, and you aren't going to like it. But if you are a realist and you can deal with facts, you may love me after I tell you. I am one who likes these numbers. I am a detailing warrior. When I figured out these numbers it was like I'd put on my BMMA (business mixed martial arts) gear and took on my competition. I first took out the weak, while mounting a quality-level attack on the major detailers. I concentrated on being the go-to guy, the local detailing expert, and I worked our referral system like a Samurai works his sword.

Are you ready for a shocker? Many of you may be thinking that the driving population uses detailing services all the time. They don't, and the numbers prove it. Some industry organizations state that 10 percent of the driving population have their automobiles detailed on a regular basis. Wrong!

This number is tainted because it includes car wash and dealership "quick detail" and their level of service and prices cannot be matched by you and me—there is no profit in it. Many times car washes and dealerships use buff and shine machines, or flood the car with a staff the size of a small army. The average detailing company will never have machines and a large staff. You do not want this model for all the tea in China, as all you would be doing is working to make payroll each week. This service model is for "non-car people," meaning that these are not your ideal customers; they want fast and cheap—real cheap!

If you are offering entry-level detailing, let's say under the $200 mark, you could average that 5 percent of the vehicles in your market are open to your level of detailing.

For those offering higher-level detailing, the real numbers are even lower. For mid-range detailing, the $250 to $400 mark, you are looking at 2 to 3 percent of the total vehicle demographics for your area. For those going after the high-end market, you are looking at 1 to 2 percent. Now some are thinking, "Wow, that stinks!" For me, I like those numbers. I am a niche guy and I love businesses with strong niche opportunities. Niches allow you to distance yourself from the other guys. And since most people are freaked out about starting such niche businesses, most in detailing are clueless to the fact that niches make it easer for their businesses to take customers away from competitors.

The best part is I don't need to trash talk my competition. I just go in, do my job, get connected, and get them thinking about me and not their business. While I am building up my brand, they are usually self-destructing.

Niche it and stay clear of what the other guys are doing. Build your business around what sells, what brings you profits, and what makes both you and your customer base happy.

Use a Microscope and Find the Perfect Clients

When I evaluate a market, I look at its general economic health, the level of vehicles within the market, and how good of a job the current detailers are doing within the market. I do not look at the total driver count but the total number of automobiles. I then use 1 to 2 percent of the total number of automobiles and divide that number by the number of detailers in the market.

Example
100,000 automobiles in my market.
Due to the good health of the market, I estimate that 2 percent of the market is detail-service based and that I can reasonably attract that level of client base. Divide that 2,000 by 12, if there are 12 detailers in the market, and that means that if I play it right and go at it hard, I could gain a total of 167 detailing clients.

That is plenty of customers if you work a good back-door sales system and offer incredible service. Matter of fact, it could be difficult to manage even if it sounds like a small total number of clients. I would rather serve fewer clients at a much higher level than serve a huge pool of clients with mediocre service. Detailing is a service business, and if you take aim at a high level of service, you don't need thousands of clients.

Setting Up Your Business with the Right Business Structure and Equipment

If you are a new home-based business owner and this is your first time setting up a business, the task can be daunting. Starting a business is far more involved than most believe it to be and there are many steps that need to be taken within the earliest days of your planned business. These steps include:

- Finding an attorney to help with issues such as corporate structure and invoice verbage.
- Locating a good accountant (CPA) is very important and will allow you to keep your finances in order from day one.
- Will you need a city, county, or state license to operate? Most commonly, the cities you operate within will require a business license.
- Check on water usage in your area. Some cities, counties, or even entire states can have water restrictions for detailers. What are the regulators saying in your area and what steps do you need to take?

Record Keeping

Record keeping is much more than simply keeping your books in order. Record keeping should involve several steps and types of record keeping:

- Keeping and Filing Receipts—As a business owner, you need to save every receipt from every purchase you make. These receipts are your proof of purchase and having them are a must for the tax man. There may be purchases you are not allowed to deduct, but let your tax advisor tell you that. I keep them all, just in case.
- Tracking Estimates—In the early days of your business, tracking estimates will be easy as you will not be giving out a high volume of them. As you grow and succeed in your detailing business, the number of estimates you provide could be daunting, and logging every estimate will be a challenge.
- Invoicing—You are going to need to keep track of invoices, both paid and unpaid. Keeping good invoicing records is not an option, it's a must. They need to be kept for tax reasons, and to help you track sales and profits (see appendix B for a sample invoice).

- Software—There are all kinds of software and systems out there today. Quickbooks is by far the standard and it is user-friendly for your accountant. Make sure you talk to your accountant about properly setting up your ledger.
- Specialized Programs—Another cool system is zenware.com. This site's online software has been developed specifically for professional detailers and is great for tracking much or all of the above. Check it out!

Taxes and Detailing

One of the first steps you should do is to contact and establish a relationship with a CPA. Ask important questions such as:

- Should I incorporate, form an LLC, or be a sole proprietor?
- Do I need to charge taxes on the work I perform and if so, at what rate?
- How do I go about hiring staff?
- How do I pay the staff?
- What about payroll taxes and obtaining workers' compensation insurance?
- Will I need to charge a tax for labor?
- Should I pay my taxes quarterly or yearly?
- Do I need to pay taxes on products and equipment I buy from out of state?

There are some real tax benefits to being in business, but only if you build the right type of business for your circumstances.

The 1099 Contractor in Detailing

This is one of the most misunderstood situations in detailing. To establish a relationship with someone who is helping you, and call them a 1099 contractor, has been challenged time and time again. In nine out of ten cases, the IRS and state tax boards hammer detailing business owners and many are put out of business from the investigation.

Will You Be A Sole Proprietor, LLC, or Corporation?

Depending on your situation, like your state tax code, there are advantages to incorporating your new business as a C, S, LLC, or a partnership corporation. It may be that a sole proprietorship structure may be best for you. To better understand corporate structures and sole proprietorships, let's discuss these options. Below are definitions of each level of business entity.

Sole Proprietor

A sole proprietorship, also known as the sole trader or simply a proprietorship, is a type of business entity owned and run by one individual and in which there is no legal distinction between the owner and the business. The owner receives all profits (subject to taxation specific to the business) and has unlimited responsibility for all losses and debts. Every asset of the business is owned by the proprietor and all debts of the business are the proprietor's. This means that the owner has no less liability than if they were acting as an individual instead of as a business. Many times, this is the type of organization detailing businesses establish and in my experience, the most common in the industry.

Limited Liability Company (LLC)

A limited liability company is, I believe, the wisest option for detailing businesses. While a business entity, an LLC is a type of unincorporated association and is not a true corporation. An LLC is often more flexible than a corporation, and therefore very friendly for small businesses such as detailing businesses that have a single owner.

For those working on high-end vehicles, forming an LLC is a smart move, as this can separate you from your actual business and some of the liabilities you face. While we are talking "high-end," let's face it, with new pickup trucks costing upward of $60,000 today, you are working on high-end vehicles no matter what you may think. An LLC could offer you an additional element of protection from loss. Talk to your CPA and/or attorney in detail about the option of forming an LLC.

C and S Corporation

If you are thinking big, a C or S corporation may be in your plans, but do so knowing this level of formation is for the big boys of business and can be a royal pain in the butt to maintain. Procedures vary widely state by state. All states that I know of require payment of a fee upon incorporation, and just the formation can be expensive and involved, much more so than a simple LLC. Within both a C and S corporation, the amount of record-keeping is greatly increased as can be the need for filing state forms. Again, if you are a large-scale car wash or mega-sized detailing business, this might not be a concern, but for the home-based, small business, a C or S corp is a big step with a great degree of advanced record-keeping.

You can see that a C or S corporation is very involved, and that depth of demand is good reason that most entering or expanding within detailing stick

Employee Identification Number (EIN)

As you start to think about your business and its future, little things are going to pop up that may be new to you, and an Employee Identification Number, or EIN, is going to be one of them. Here is what the IRS website says about EINs: "An Employer Identification Number (EIN) is also known as a Federal Tax Identification Number, and is used to identify a business entity. Generally, businesses need an EIN."

If you are going to form a Corporation, LLC, or hire staff, you will need an EIN for sure. Many times, if you are paying to have your Corporation or LLC formed, the organization forming such will apply for an EIN for you. If you are forming your own Corporation or LLC, you can apply for the EIN online by following the directions on the IRS site. The site, www.irs.gov, has a great deal of information on EINs, so I urge you to go check that site out and be informed.

with either the Sole Proprietor or the LLC options because of their ease in maintaining both.

I would strongly suggest that you talk with your CPA about how you should best set up and establish your new business and how to best incorporate your business, giving you the most shelter from taxes and liabilities.

Insurance

General Liability Insurance—This type of insurance is most common but attached to that insurance, as a business working on automobiles, you also need garagekeepers insurance. This type of insurance covers any damages that come from your efforts while detailing a client's automobiles. This is the name/type of policy you want to look for. I have found that Travelers Insurance is detailing friendly.

- Workers' Compensation Insurance—As your business grows and expands, the need to hire staff will become a must and you will need to obtain workers' compensation insurance. Each state runs its workers' comp differently. Some states have their own workers' comp plans while others open up workers comp to outside insurance organizations. Just to be clear, if you have staff helping you, workers' comp insurance is not an option, it's a must-have policy. Check with your local state employment office or your CPA for more details.

- Health Insurance—One of the biggest struggles I, and many of those I have trained and mentored over the years, have had is health insurance. I know how expensive insurance is today. But I want to stress that detailing is a profession where you can get hurt and you need to carry health insurance for yourself and your family members. If you get hurt, sick, or are struck down with an illness and don't have insurance, it can cost you your business. In addition, when you hire staff, think about providing health insurance for them. Doing so can add real value to the job you offer and be a motivator for good detailers to stay with you.

- Supplemental Health Insurance—We have all seen the Aflac commercials on TV with the duck yelling "Aflac," but do you know what Aflac and other companies offer? Supplemental insurance, such as what Aflac offers, pays a cash benefit to the insured. The amount of cash and how it is paid out depends on the supplemental health insurance plan or policy. Some popular supplemental policies are specific disease insurance for cancer, accidental death and dismemberment, accident health insurance, and hospital indemnity insurance.

■ Life Insurance—If you are young and single with no kids, health insurance may not be important to you. For those who are married and/or have children, you need to think about obtaining a solid life insurance policy. Here are a few reasons why:

1. If you were to die, who will provide for your family?
2. In the event you pass, you do not want your family taking on debt that you and your business may have.
3. Are you the money maker in the family? If so, if something were to happen to you, how would your family make ends meet?

There are many things to think about when taking out a life insurance policy. You need to consult with your family life insurance provider to cover what you and your family needs are.

■ Specialty Insurance—If you are going to offer specialty services on aircraft, boats, and RVs, these services may require additional insurance. Of these, aircraft services will require that you obtain hangarkeepers insurance. These specialty policies are not cheap but are needed to cover your liabilities for the special services you are offering.

Dealing With City, County, and State

Make sure to check with your local, county, and state labor and business departments to see if you need any special licensing or other permits. Here are a few examples of what city, county, and state licenses and/or permits you may encounter:

City business license—If you are mobile, this may include every city you operate within. Each city is different and you will need to do your homework.

Special water permit—Some cities require those working with water to take out special water usage or water disposal permits.

Home-based business license—Yes, that's right, some area government agencies today even charge you for working out of your home. Some states will require that you inform them of a new business, so make sure to check with your state's tax and business departments.

Signage fees—If you are going to start a shop, a fixed shop, even on property you own, the city or county could have fees associated with signage. Check with your local city and or county.

The Role Credit Card Processing Plays In Detailing

This day and age, you are nuts not to accept credit and debit cards. I know there are people who don't accept plastic, but it does limit the attraction to your customer base.

Worst case, sign up for PayPal and send your customers an electronic invoice. This allows them to use plastic and it's easy for you to perform. You can even get PayPal Mobile and invoice them right from their front doorstep.

In today's world, you can process credit cards right from your phone. You can use a call-in service where you call in the customer's information and the card is processed.

There are phone-mounted credit card processors you can buy for your smartphone, and I am telling you, this is not only a convenience for your customers, but the image it creates of you being cutting edge is worth the investment alone!

What I Wish I Had Known Before I Started My Business

Jim Goguen
Jim's Auto Installations & Detailing Center
Ipswich, MA

I wish I had known a little more about business and the inner workings of a business, such as accounting, payroll, and long-term projections. Starting out at the age of twenty, taking a hobby and passion and turning it into my sole income without any planning, was extremely tough to do. When starting out, figuring out how much money I would need to bring in weekly seemed very simple. I would just calculate what my bills would be monthly and divide by four. Seems simple until you need to factor in overhead, operating costs, taxes, and the biggest problem, slow times. At some point it would have been a better move for me to have taken a small business or accounting course. Another thing that would have helped out when first starting a detailing business in New England would have been preparing for the winter months and slow seasons.

Home-Based Office Space and Equipment

A home-based business today is not only rewarding, it's fun. Think of all the cool tools aside from your detailing equipment you can have at your disposal. As you start or expand your business, here are some of the tools that will help within your home-based business. Owning a detailing business is not just about the detailing aspects. I have some great tech toys within the business, and I have access to them twenty-four hours a day. Many times, these tools are tax deductible!

Computer

I am not here to sell you on computers but I am here to point you in the right direction. I am going be direct: Three years ago I switched to a Macintosh laptop for my business and it was one of the best steps ever I took. Why Mac?

- The creative suite that Mac offers is incredible. Mac makes designing support materials for your business easier and much more creative than a standard PC. You can convert flyers, bids, and support materials into PDFs in a snap with no additional downloads. The templates Mac offers are incredible and the drop-in option for photos is a nice tool that allows you to look like a true pro!
- Video marketing will be much easier. Video is a key to marketing and iMovie makes producing your videos much easier.
- I love Keynote on my Mac, it makes producing presentations a breeze.

A PC is a good tool, I used one for years, but I am 100 percent vested in this statement: If you are buying a computer for your business, go Mac.

Land Line or Cell

If you are mobile and very stable and plan on keeping your number for a very long time, there is no reason a cell line won't work for your business. The issue with cells is that if you grow into a fixed location or you are starting out as a fixed location, you may wish to have a land line. If you are a fixed location and want a monitored alarm system for your building, you are going to need a land line anyway.

A Virtual Phone System

For those times when you can't answer the phone, you have some really cool options in the form of virtual phone systems. These systems can deliver a very professional sound and image of your business for those making contact with you via phone. Here are a few of those systems and what they offer:

- Grasshopper—This service will do many things, including voice mail, a toll-free number, and a long list of benefits, including sending your voice mails via e-mail.
- Google Voice—A nice tool that can add many useful tools to your current land line, cell line, or both. Go check it out.
- The Smartphone—I have an entire section on smartphones but want to mention that today's smartphones are in reality offering many of the same benefits as a virtual phone system, making the value of a smartphone smart for your business.

What a Smartphone Can Do For Your Detailing Business

Smartphones are everywhere in today's world. I mean, why not want a phone that is more powerful than the computers NASA used in the '70s? You have so much power right at your fingertips and they are just cool to have! These phones help me run my business today. Here are just a few high points. I like the Droid and iPhone systems and here is why:

- All my contacts are at my fingertips. I can use my contacts to manage my customer base.
- My schedule is instantly accessible.
- The camera included with my phone has an amazing 8 megapixels. I take all my before-and-after photos with the phone's camera.
- When I am too busy to take notes, I have a voice record app to record items such as appointments or conversations I need to remember.
- With an advanced headset, I can work and listen to music, and my head-phones act as hearing protection, all while still being able to hear my customers and/or staff, if they need something.
- The built-in GPS navigation is also amazing. Nice to have for us mobile guys.
- The detailing industry-specific software is great for customer management, invoicing, and customer service reminders. There are new apps being offered every day.
- I use my phone for up to 50 percent of my online social media marketing efforts.

iPads and Tablets

Do you want a cutting-edge menu design? Make your menu on a tablet like the iPad and you are going to sell some details. I love the iPad for showing customers expectation videos. Videos showing vehicles before and after detailing are great sales tools. Here is the future now for iPads and tablets:

- Can be used for processing credit cards.
- Can use detailing software right on the device and manage customer information.
- Both photos and video are important to use for documenting your work, abilities, and to promote business. Today's iPad or tablet can take photos and video clips alike.
- I think the image and lasting value of you using these tools within your detailing business can do a good job of separating you from your competitors, and build up your perceived value within your market.

Using A Multifunction Machine In Your Home Office Gives You All You Need

With modern technologies the need for office machinery is almost nonexistent. But I do find that I need a copier and printer almost daily. So why not buy a multifunction printer (MFP) that houses a copier, printer, fax machine, and scanner all in one? I have owned these units for the past twelve plus years and I prefer the HP and Canon small-office MFPs. Also think about complete digital, online options such as Efax and others.

Now that you have your business structure in place and your home office set up, let's move on to the part you have been waiting for—what products you will need to deliver that shine!

Equipping Your Detailing Business

Detailing equipment and product manufacturers are providing the professional detailer an arsenal of weapons that assist us in wowing our customers in less time. Today's detailing products are more effective, easier to use, and allow us to gain better results faster, meaning our industry has the opportunity to earn profits at much higher levels than just two or three years ago.

Your equipment and product needs will need to be carefully laid out and in the beginning setting up your equipment and products list is tough. Buying detailing products local is great, but in reality, the items you are going to need are hard to find locally. If I could, I would buy every item I need locally to support the local business, but many of the items you are going to need as a pro level detailer are very specialized. You could go with store-purchased products but what you buy over the counter versus pro grade detailing products is night and day. If you are going to be a true pro, you need true pro-level detailing products.

- There are several suppliers and a couple of them are very dedicated to the pro-level detailer.
- Autogeek (www.autogeek.net)—This site is one of the biggest and most respected within the detailing industry. Autogeek has a massive following and is led by two great guys. Max, the owner, is the bomb and my buddy, and Mike is the training director and an over-the-top detailer when it comes to skills and knowledge.
- Auto Detailing Solutions (www.autodetailingsolutions.net)—Owner Rick is a great guy and very dedicated to us pro-level detailers. He is very helpful and runs a small, yet highly effective detailing supply company.

- The Detail Boss (www.detailboss.com)—This is a very boutique-based site that carries a very specialized and small number of products and only the latest in detailing equipment. The site is organized and run by detailers, for detailers.

While the above sites carry a wide variety of products, there are countless specialized products needed for your business that are all available directly from various manufacturers' websites. Having a one-stop-shop online is simply not real world as there are new and exciting product developments weekly.

On page 90, please find a chart of sample items you will need for your detailing business.

Fixed Location

Laying out an effective fixed location is not as easy as it may seem. You really need to hire a consultant to assist you. But, if you are going to design a shop on your own here are some items to think about.

The Size and Location of Your Shop

Many times, I see people setting up their first shop, and it's simply too big. You need to think of the true space you are going to use and the volume you will be experiencing. Most of my shops have been in the 1,000- to 1,500-square-foot size, and I loved the small size. My largest shop was just shy of 4,000 square feet, and it was just too large and too expensive. Let's talk about location. Drive-by exposure is important, but what you pay for that exposure versus the return on the investment needs to be looked at and looked at hard. Some of you may be in an area where you have an outbuilding or garage that could house your detailing business. Not everyone is open to this situation and it does have both benefits and drawbacks.

If you have an outbuilding or garage that you can work out of your expenses (overhead) could greatly be reduced with this option. You do need to address a couple of realities within this however such as:

1. What is your customer's opinion? In the early days, having someone come to a residential property may be a perceived value nightmare.
2. You need to consider how nice your property looks. Does it look professional?
3. Is it convenient for the customer? Is the property close to your customer base?
4. Will the city or county allow you to set up your business at this location?

5. Homeowner associations can be nasty about home-based business, so make sure this will not be an issue if you have a homeowners association.

6. I love working from home and have had two home-based shops. On the other hand, it made escaping work challenging at times. I had to set business hours for myself and agreed with my wife and kids to not escape back to work unless it was during those hours.

The Monthly Cost versus the Proposed Income

I am going to keep this simple: A sizable overhead will KILL YOUR BUSINESS! Overhead is all your costs for doing business—equipment, supplies, cost of doing business, marketing, sales support, utilities, and anything that keeps a business going. In today's world, keep your bills in check and don't rack up debt. Period. Here is a list of overhead items that can sneak up on you, so you need to think about these items:

- Marketing Expenses—It shocks me to see what unknowing detailing professionals spend on marketing and the lack of return they realize on those marketing efforts.
- Insurance—You're going to need various levels of insurance from health to business.
- Utilities—If you run a shop at home or away from home, keeping the lights and heat on will cost you.
- Staff—Of all the expenses you could experience that can make or break your business, your staffing expenses are something you need to know and understand. If your man-hours are too high and your staff costs are not in check, this could hurt your business in a very bad way. On the flip side, not having enough staff can also hurt as you do not want to turn business away to other detailing businesses because you are making customers wait too long for your services. Knowing and understanding your staffing needs is very important.
- Fuel—If you are starting a mobile business, think about fuel usage and thus the vehicle you use for your mobile unit. I encourage you to think smaller than traditional and go with an eco-based mobile detailing system.

The Layout

Laying out an effective shop is not difficult when you first start up, as the volume you experience won't push you that hard in the early days. What is most important is equipping your shop properly. Again, you can turn to an industry consultant or look at www.detailingsuccess.com for more ideas.

Your Mobile System

If you are going mobile, the first thing people think about is trailers or big vans. Can I challenge you to think out of the box? As I write this, gas is very expensive and the price is not going down. Today's detailing systems can be fit into smaller, more economical vehicles.

Pickup Truck

If you already own a pickup truck, add on a shell and a few neat system tools and you could have a nice system. Add on a vehicle wrap and you have a moving billboard.

Trailers

Trailers can be tough to navigate in tight areas and if you are in an upscale area, sometimes the driveways we need to navigate are small and tight and a trailer is not, in my opinion, the best way to go. I won't go as far as saying there is no way I would go with a trailer or large van, but in 99.9 times out of 100, I would go with a smaller, fuel-efficient system.

New Age Mobile Systems

I am all over these smaller, more economical mobile detailing units. I have assisted in building mobile detailing systems on vehicles such as the Chevy HHR Cargo Crossover, the Ford Transit Van, and a host of other small, yet highly effective mobile platforms.

Equipment

Odds are you have researched detailing equipment ranging from items for your home-based shop, your retail shop, and/or your mobile detailing system. But the day-to-day equipment you will be using is important to think about and I encourage you to expand your line of thinking when it comes to the detailing equipment. There are many tools that are not common with most detailers and that is why true success is so uncommon with most detailers. You need to be free thinking and cutting edge to be the best.

High-Speed Polishers

As I write this book, this is a real hot topic within the industry. Until recently, the high-speed polisher, also known as the rotational polisher, has been the big daddy of a professional detailer's arsenal. The high-speed polisher has also stirred fears among new detailers and has caused many sleepless nights with worry and concern over damaging paint finishes.

High-speed polishers have their place in detailing. I have performed thousands of details with high-speed correction techniques, and I still use high-speed polishers, but not very often.

These days, there are better ways of paint perfection for the average automobile detailer and I have spent the past three years achieving absolute paint perfection utilizing the modern-day forced-action polisher. In this book I am not going to make many plugs, but the Flex XC3401 has been a game changer.

I still teach the art of high-speed polishing but I spend 80 percent more time teaching the art of modern-day paint perfection.

Today, I perform $2,000 to $50,000 details and rarely touch a high-speed polisher. These are a variety of vehicles ranging from mild to wild, yet my quality is better, I get the job done faster, and thus my profits are up. The really good news is, I have been able to perform at this high level all while removing less healthy clear coat than I had in the days I strictly used the high-speed polisher.

High-speed polishing is mostly used by those old dogs like me who perform high-end work. I have found that if those professionals would dedicate the time to learning a new skill with the forced action, they too would see the benefits of the new generation of tooling., Most old dogs won't take the time to learn the skills, so my message to you is not to fall into that trap as a new pro detailer. Keep an open mind.

Forced-Action Polishers

One tool immediately comes to mind, the Flex XC3401, and with good reason. I was a skeptic when I first learned of this tool. After spending a couple hundred hours with the 3401, I was shocked at this tool's capabilities and was eager to expand my knowledge of it even further. This tool is the best of both worlds with the capabilities of a true rotational polisher while having the finishing abilities of a DA, all mixed into one polisher.

Now, not everyone shares my opinion of this tool or will agree with me on its capabilities, but those are usually the same people who have a fraction of the time on this machine. What convinced me that the 3401 was truly a very capable tool was what I was able to achieve on bare aluminum. Paint correction is a true art while aluminum polishing and finishing is the highest level of artful detailing one can accomplish, and the 3401 changed they way I compound, polish, and finish both aluminum and paint alike.

Of all the tools to enter the detailing industry in the past decade or so, the true forced-action polisher has made a large impact on the profitability of progressive shops.

Not only can I get out heavy imperfections, I can do it faster, all while removing less of the healthy paint system. Also, these tools reduce the learning curve for absolute paint perfection and make burning paint a tad more difficult. Burning paint

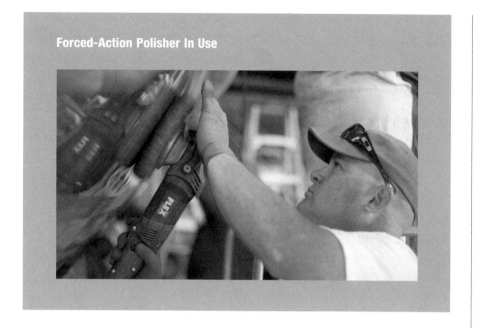

Forced-Action Polisher In Use

is bad—very bad—and now pro detailers have a new tool to make detailing more profitable and achieving high levels of outcome easier.

European Steam

The best development for detailing professionals in the past two decades is the steamer! Undoubtedly, this tool has changed detailing for those who have taken the time to learn the art. This tool is used on both interiors and exteriors alike, but are far more useful on interiors. I would NEVER detail without my steamer. Period.

Would you agree that time is money? Would you also agree that getting a car REALLY clean is important in your detailing business? This is what using steam is all about! Less than 5 percent of pro detailers utilize steam. A good unit is right at the $1,000 mark and most won't invest at that level. WARNING: Steam is only as good as the technician. Don't think you can simply buy a steamer and start using it. There is a learning curve and you need to learn how to best use steam correctly before you realize the big rewards steam can offer. Here are all of the places you can effectively use steam in your detailing:

Door Panels, Vents, Cup Holders, Dashes, and All the Nooks and Crannies

In the past you would have a nice tray of various brushes and cleaners neatly laid out and carefully choose each brush for each tight nook on the dash, door panel, and tight areas within the car. You would add stiffer brushes for heavily soiled areas, such as speaker covers covered in coffee or sticky soda. But that was so yesterday.

Today, we use steam, more importantly, European steam. What would take one, two, or three hours, now takes minutes to complete. The system outlined with brushes is sexy but the main idea about that system I want you to understand is that steam cleans better, with no or little chemicals, and it is faster. Ever heard the term time is money? Well steam means more money in your pocket at the end of the day—and happier customers.

Carpets and Stains

When it comes to cleaning carpets, most within the detailing industry are stuck in 1975, using wet extraction. Steam is safer, faster, dries more quickly, and offers a better level of clean on carpets. In addition, we can remove stains within carpet faster and with less chemicals which offers a safer, more eco-friendly detail for customers and allows you to build up your reputation as well as man-hour profits.

Upholstery and Sport Fabrics

A steam system can remove up to 90 percent of the stains you come across as a detailer. New automobiles with a cloth interior option have had sport seating materials in the fabric for the past five years or so. This fabric is terrible to deal with. It is subject to water stains from contact with your body (sweat) and quickly absorbs anything dropped on the surface. Getting the related stains out of these modern-day fabrics is nearly impossible. Many within detailing are still stuck on wet extraction, which entails injecting water onto and into the upholstery, then extracting it, or at least attempting to. The issue, in most cases, is that surfaces and undersurfaces are so wet, that two, three, or four days later, the stains reappear. This is called rewicking or wicking.

Wicking is a very common problem for those who use extraction, especially as they are getting the upholstery and carpets really wet. The carpets and upholstery look great when they are done. But over the following days the stains reappear. Sometimes lightly but often within three to twelve days, the stains resurface almost to the point they were before. With steam, if you are using it correctly, you will have zero wicking. And the seats and carpets are dry by the time you return the vehicle to your customer. Steam allows you to see true, real-world results and deliver incredible quality, all while making money and, more importantly, allowing you to build a long list of happy customers.

Red Stains

You have seen the cars, they look more like the inside of a Kool-Aid manufacturing plant than they do a car, and those red stains are nasty to get out, even with steam. But, steam allows you to get 80 to 90 percent more of the red stain out then extraction and is faster. We upsell our red stain removal and make a nice profit from getting these nasty stains out. The key is using the right chemicals along with steam.

Leather

If you have dirty leather, steam deep cleans leather and saves you time while increasing your overall quality.

Headliners

Can you keep a secret? Despite what the "desk jockey" industry know-it-alls say, steam works great on headliners—as long as you play by the rules and know what you are doing. I have over 5,000 cleaned headliners under my belt. But don't tell those other, uneducated detailers how easy it is to make extra money from this step. It's our secret.

Odor Removal Assistance

One of the keys to odor removal is getting as much of the cause out of the car, and steam plays a huge part in that.

Exterior Clean Up of Gunk, Wax Around Emblems, and Trim

When you start detailing, you will realize that your paint correction products grow legs and crawl into every tight spot you can find. Steam makes easy work of removing residue from the tightest areas.

Wheels

Most of the time, we get the wheels clean during the wash process. In cases where you are using eco-based detailing systems, the steamer can be a huge bonus. Additionally, if you have a car where the lug nut area is a mess, the steam makes easy work of this tedious chore.

High-End Engine Compartments

One word: liability. When it comes to working on the engine compartments of high-end vehicles, you will not see me put water on that engine. I prefer the steam with much more control and grace for this job and the owners of exotics will love you for it.

Dual-Action Polishers

Dual actions have come a long way in the last couple years. I view these machines as more pro-amateur tools than pro-level tools. But if you have a helper and just want a tool for your unskilled help to wax a car, these are nice entry-level tools for that purpose. If it were me, I'd stick with the forced-action machines.

Wet Extractors

This is old technology. You can buy a box-store shop vac but you are going to need an extractor. Or you can purchase a hybrid shop vac and have both a shop vac and extractor in one. If you have a fixed location and can go with a central extractor system that co-brands as a vacuum that is a different story. Central systems are powerful and many are capable of acting as both a vac and an extractor in one.

Hybrid Shop Vacuums and Dry Extraction

By far, the best way to go, especially if you are mobile or don't have the funds for a central system. Look for the highest lift in inches you can find.

Ozone

We have used both CD- and UV-based ozone for years and still do, but the new bio-technologies are looking very attractive. Ozone has some health concerns and can be corrosive, but up until recent times, has been the go-to within a complete odor elimination system.

New Biotechnologies

As I write this, I am testing a variation of bio systems for odor removal and this technology has come a long way in the past couple years. It is now getting affordable enough for detailers to use within their operations. I like these systems due to the fact that they are safe for humans, animals, and the interior surfaces of vehicles. They are highly effective at truly removing odors and not simply masking them. These systems can quickly and effectively remove pet, smoke, food, and other odors, germs, bacteria, mold, mildew, stains, and other contaminants from the interior. The system is a revolutionary and environmentally friendly odor, germ, and allergen removal system that works on cars, boats, and RVs. The systems are very useful and marketable within these industries:

- Auto Dealers
- Car Auctions
- Car Washes
- RV Dealerships
- Fleets
- Municipalities

Detailing Clay

I wanted to bring this out in the clear and within a separate category. Clay has been around for nearly two decades now and is still not taken seriously by some that are new to detailing. Folks, clay is a staple within any and all detailing businesses, or at least it should be.

Detailer Tip

Clay today comes in various forms such as moderate clay, aggressive clay, clay sponges, and now, clay towels. Most commonly used clays are soft bars of moldable clay that can be used to remove surface debris such as environmental fallout, rail dust, and other paint-surface debris that can affect the overall health and shine of the entire paint system on a vehicle.

Various Cleaners and Dressings

You are going to need a long list of general products for detailing. There are many products out there that do more than just one job. For instance, I have found a degreaser that works as a bug remover also. Getting multiuse products saves you money and keeps us sane, as one could go crazy ordering all the needed products.

Interior Products	Exterior Products	Equipment/Supplies
Automotive All Purpose Cleaner (APC)	Compound	Forced Action Polisher
Leather Cleaner	Polishing Compound	150 Rotational Polisher
Leather Conditioner	DA Polish	3" DA polisher
Carpet Cleaner	Polishes	Hybrid Vacuum/Extraction System
Stain Removal Product Kit	Fine Polishes	Wool Pads
Magic Erasers	Sealers	Microfiber Pads
Cleaning Brushes	Spray Applied Sealer	Foam Pads
Popsicle Sticks	Color Enhancement Top Coat	Detailing Steamer
Water Based Dressing	Clays	Spare Backing Plates
Protective Dressing	Clay Sponge	Pad Washer
Carpet Stain Tool	Surface Prep Towel	Paint Gauge
Headliner Comb	Inspection Light	Paint Inspection Light
Suede Cleaner	Tire Covers	Dressing Applicator Pads
Interior Detailing Light	Wash Shampoo	Bucket System
Stain Removal Pads	Wash Mitts	Pad Cart
Carpet Cleaning Towels	Drying Towels	Pad Washer
Microfiber Towels	Adhesive Remover	Interior Odor/Purification System
Dog Hair Stone	Blue/Green Masking Tape	Extension Cords
Window Cleaning Tool	Microfiber Towel SetXC	A solid camera for before/after photos & video

The difference between a wax and a sealer in a nutshell? Waxes are infamous for having carnauba in them as the main ingredient. Carnauba is a product supplied to us from Mother Nature and has been used over the centuries as a wax for a host of surfaces. For many years, carnauba was a detailer's best friend. Today, sealers are widely available, more durable, and, in most cases of detailing, offer just as high a level of shine as a carnauba wax. That level of shine is a debatable statement in many circles but note sealers today are a very desirable way to protect a vehicle's paint system.

Compounds, Polishes, Paint-Protection Products, and Color-Enhancement Products

This is where people go completely nuts and spend way too much money. Paint correction is an addiction and I have dealt with it for years. I often tell people that "today is a great day to be in detailing." The equipment and products have never been this good and have never made detailing as simple as it is today. In my shop right now for retail work, I have a total of eight paint-correction, paint-polishing, paint-protection, and paint-enhancement products. These products are made up of compounds; the heavy correction products and polishes that define and bring perfection to the clear coat; the fine polishes used to bring depth and brilliance to the paint; and the sealers and/or waxes that can both protect the paint and enhance its color and overall look.

Paint Gauges, Paint Microscopes, and Paint Inspection Lights

Everyone gets all hung up on paint polishing, and therefore paint perfection, but before you go there, you need to tool up and invest in the things that will make you perform and look the part of a professional detailer. Paint gauges measure the total paint system. The high-end gauges will give you the exact thickness of the clear coat, which is what we are most concerned with. Paint microscopes, paint inspection lights, and even reflective gauges are all useful tools.

- Paint Microscopes—These allow you to look at imperfections up close and personal. They will assist you in learning what you can and cannot remove, and enable you to examine imperfections within the clear coat both before your correction efforts and after.

- Paint Inspection Lights—These paint inspection lights come in three flavors:

  1. Handheld
  2. Work Stand-Based Inspection Lights
  3. Hard Mounted Work Lights

- Paint Gauges—I have owned many and this is a tool I do not like to go cheap on. Call (248) 292-5710 or (800) 334-2843 and ask them about the ETG-2 and let them know Renny sent you. I love these meters.
- Gloss Meters (GM)—There are two camps on the topic of gloss meters. One side supports the use of GM and insists that these tools are accurate. From my relationships with people like Jason Rose of Meguiar's, I think GMs alone are not accurate. In addition, most detailers will rarely use this tool. Only the top-level detailers working on very exotic vehicles will use these tools and even then, they're rare, even in the elite groups of the detailing industry.

Eco-Based Detailing Is Real and Growing

Not all that long ago, eco detailing was a joke among pro detailers. Today, waterless and low-volume washing are gaining popularity. Regulations at the federal, state, county, and local city levels are catapulting these washing and detailing options into reality. Even localized business parks and commercial locations are banning traditional washing methods, making the eco-based detailing methods a reality in professional detailing today and in the future.

> Choose a job you love, and you will never have to work a day in your life.
>
> —*Confucius*

Eco-Mobile Detailing

Here is an example of an eco-based mobile detailing unit.

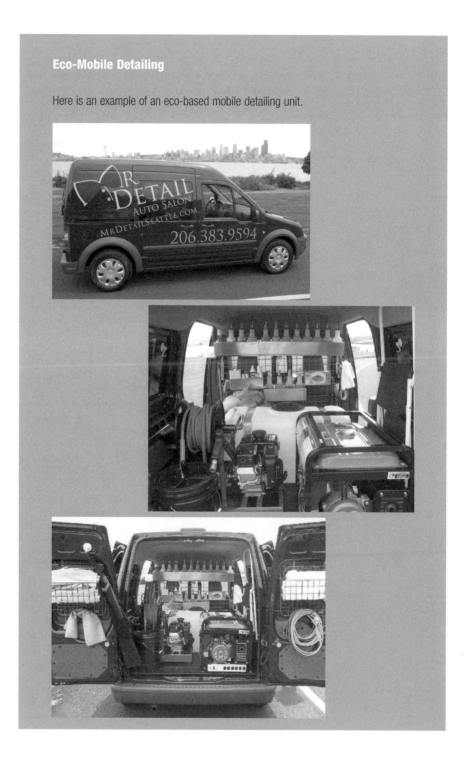

You work on your car all day and when you are done, you are blown away by how great it looks. You detail for family, friends, and neighbors and they are also amazed. That type of weekend venture has launched more detailing careers than I can count. In good part, my own career started with similar, passion-based beginnings, so I want to share some facts about transitioning from a hobby detailer to a paid, pro-level detailer:

- When you step out the door of amateur detailing, and into the ring of pro-level detailing, an entire new world of expectations arise. Expectations from customers and profit expectations are real.
- You are getting paid for detailing now, and learning on the job is not impossible, but the likelihood of you realizing true success is minimal.
- You are going to be facing off with pro detailers that are hungry like you: pros who have been doing it longer, are connected, and may or may not know what they are doing.
- You are going to be facing off with detailers that are looking for the same customers as you are.
- You are going to be competing with others to keep lifetime customers from jumping ship and going to the other guys such as you. They want those lifelong customers just like you do and they are going to fight you.

They have an edge on you. They have experience, time in the market, and, good or bad, they have a reputation. Now, the great majority of detailing businesses are easy prey to a sharp, business-based detailing pro who is also a master at relationship building. You can win the business, but if you don't know what you are doing in detailing and are not able to perform at a very high level, all the business skills in the world are not going to to save you. Combining business skills with detailing abilities is where true success can be found.

You Need to Perform at a Very High Level

Detailing at a high level means more than one would think. Performing at a high level means that you act in a professional fashion, responsible and dedicated to performing detailing correctly. If you got this far in this book, I want you to commit to me right now that you are dedicated to the integrity of detailing, far more than those you will be competing with in your market. When you detail with integrity, you not only bring yourself up, you lift the entire industry up.

- Those who perform and thus succeed at the highest levels within detailing know, understand, and do a great job of evaluating a vehicle's needs. This level of detailer understands how to look at paint and know what can be achieved with his or her skills. Successful detailers design a profit-based menu based on their local market's expectations and pricing ceilings.
- High-level detailing professionals understand the science regarding paint correction and paint perfection.
- Successful detailers track man-hour performance and know when to say when.
- Those operating at the highest level do so with a detailer's creed whereas we cause no harm. The vehicles we work on at this level can be time capsules of automobile history. These are rare or very exotic vehicles that the day-to-day detailer has no business working on.
- Successful detailers sell upfront and explain the outcome results versus the customer's budget. Remember the old saying, "You get what you pay for."
- Those who desire the highest levels of success understand both wet and dry sanding. These steps take the advanced skills that are needed and should not be taken lightly. Sanding is an artistic part of detailing. The sanding itself is not difficult, sanding while not depleting healthy clear coat is where the real skills are needed, as are the skills to remove the scratch you create during the sanding process.
- Some of the most challenging aspects of detailing at this level are steps that many skip over, or fail to realize how important these steps are. They include the ability to deal with interior stains and odors, and to do so without caus-

ing damage. Interior challenges take a great deal of skill to achieve a high-level outcome.

- Successful detailers are as committed to the business of detailing, as they are to the art of detailing.

Specialized Training

We talked briefly about the skills it takes to detail and we visited some of the high-level skills that the upper levels of detailing professionals hold. Let's visit a wider range of skills you need to be educated about. Below you will read what I professionally believe you should be knowledgeable of. These are topics I cover with every single detailing student I teach, mentor, and coach.

Solid Business Foundation Building

The start of your business is the foundation of your business. This will secure positioning within your market and set you up for the success you need in today's business environment.

Detailing Science

If you are going to be a talented detailer, you need to know not only the hows of detailing but also the whys:

- Modern-day automobile paint systems.
- The paint systems of the past so you can deal with classic-based automobiles.
- Today's wet- and dry-sanding systems. Proper sanding is something that you, the successful detailer, are going to need to know and be skilled in if you expect to compete with the best in the industry.
- The makeup of modern-day compounds, polishes, waxes, sealers, and color enhancement products, and how they are made, and how they work on modern-day paint systems.
- The tools, equipment, and instruments of pro-level detailing. This is a huge part of what I teach as not all equipment is created equal. You need to be exposed to as many of the leading items as possible in detailing so you can make smart purchasing decisions.

Sales

How to perform and sell the items on your detailing menu. I am a major fan of a simple menu and my own menu contains four or five main services with a handful of a la carte services.

- The Express Detail is designed for very nicely maintained automobiles or as a maintenance detail for your existing customers.
- Stage I Detail is an entry-level detail designed for a well-maintained vehicle that needs a little help.
- The Stage II Detail is a much more technical detail than the Stage I, and takes a fair amount of skill to perform. The customer that goes with a Stage II detail will usually have some issues such as light-to-moderate scratches on the exterior and light-to-moderate stains and soils within the interiors.
- The Stage III Detail is designed for automobiles with some serious issues that you, the pro-level detailer, will need to not just be comfortable with, but highly skilled within. This level of detailing customer is looking for amazing results or is facing a vehicle finish and or interior that they have let go and they are looking to get the automobile's grandness back.
- The Concours Detail in most detailing businesses is a rare level of service. Oh, I hear many detailers bragging about these details and how they perform at this level but truth be known, few of us in the entire world can command the type of money it takes to pay for this level of detail. This level of detail is really reserved for show- or collector-level automobiles. For a daily driver to receive this level of detail is not only rare but pointless. Now, every once in a great while an owner will want this level of detail for the car he or she drives to work, and if they are willing to pay for it, what the heck? I am totally game to making their wishes a reality! Of course, you could give this level of detail away, which is what most are doing, but to make real profits, few detailers are making a living at this level of the detailing game.

You may be asking, only four or five services on my menu? Really? Well, kind of. The nice thing about a great menu such as the Stage menu I outlined is that you can separate a well-designed menu into interior, exterior, or a combo of both and come up with a simple, yet detailed menu.

In addition, you can add on additional a la carte services to enhance your menu. Here are some samples of a la carte items that you should consider for your detailing menu:

- Odor removal
- Dog hair removal
- Hard water spot removal
- Paint transfer clean up
- Heavy scratch removal
- Black trim restoration
- Deep wheel cleaning
- Wheel polishing
- Wheel sealant application
- Interior heavy stain removal
- Water damage restoration
- Water stain removal from sport seating surfaces
- Headliner cleaning

Birds of a Feather

When happy, success-based pro detailers hang out, we mentor each other and share information. Finding a group that is open is tough as most detailers think they have the world's largest secret when it comes to detailing knowledge, and they hate to share.

But if you can get tied into a group that is sharing, cutting-edge, all about the complete system of detailing, and being both business- and art-based, you will grow as both a pro and a person. Some of my best friends are right here in our industry and there are some amazing people among us! See appendix C for more information.

Finding Mentors

One of the smartest moves you will make is finding mentors. I have five mentors in my life right now, and only two are in the detailing industry. The others are big-business mentors, small-business mentors, life mentors, and guys I look up to as husbands and fathers. Mentors are key, not just in detailing, but life!

- What I look for in a mentor—I stumbled across my first mentors when I was young, but today, even in my forties, I am still on the hunt for good men-

To Do It All Over Again

Diane Doyle
Detailing Success
Big Bear Lake, CA

I graduated from the University of Oklahoma with a Bachelor of Science degree in Law Enforcement Administration. I worked for several years in the field. After starting our family, I decided it was a time for a career change. I am a detailer and the wife of a detailer. I love cars and love to bring them back to their original glory. Interiors are my specialty.

I talk to so many people and they say, "I can wash my own car, I can detail." For some, that is true, but for most it is a pipe dream. Education is key, whether it is self or formal. There are so many ways to obtain knowledge and skills. Get some formal training. Stay current on new processes, new products, new equipment, and cutting-edge techniques.

Always realize that you never stop learning. Continue to push your boundaries and evolve. The detailing industry evolves so fast and there are continually new and improved methods, products, and ideas. Don't limit yourself and your business by getting stuck in a rut. I can't count how many times I have heard, "Well, I've been detailing for twenty years and there's not much I don't know." Old dogs CAN learn new tricks. Don't get so set in your ways that you let your business stagnate.

The Internet is a wonderful tool and the information you can get is immense, but don't always believe everything you read on the web. Do your due diligence and make educated choices and decisions. With this being said, it can also be detrimental. So much of the time, people spend hours and hours surfing when that time could be spent much more wisely. Be reasonable in your time management. Set goals and limits. Be hands on. You can read, learn, and research, but detailing is hands on so practice, practice, practice!

Finally, look around you and find some mentors. Utilize those around you and learn from their mistakes. Not only can you get invaluable insight and direction, but you also get a fresh and unbiased look from an outsider's perspective. It is very easy to convince yourself that the path you are choosing is the right one. Sometimes you are so close to something that your perspective is skewed. Mentors are an amazing resource.

tors. I look for those who are realistic, willing to stand up to me, discuss the options I have, and show good judgment within their own life and business. I don't want a control freak for a mentor, I want someone who can help me grow while also growing themselves.

- Age makes a difference—I am sure you, those reading this book, are of varied ages. For you young guys and gals, look for mentors who are older and willing to help point you in the right direction. To this day, my mentors who are older and a little wiser share something with me almost daily that changes my outlook, view, or direction within a situation.

- Success-based—Find mentors who are truly successful and truly want to see you succeed.

- Life versus business—I want to be very clear about this. I have mentors within business and mentors within life, but few mentors can mentor me in both. I know who I respect business-wise and I know who I respect as husbands, fathers, and people. It's my job to separate the two and to work what they both can teach me in my life. I like to relate mentoring to shoes. I have workout shoes for the gym and I have dress shoes for the meeting. One is not better than the other; they are both simply specialized for the task at hand.

Some organizations to think about where mentors can be found:

SCORE (www.SCORE.org)—I have had mixed results with SCORE, but I know others who have made lifelong friends or mentors from dealing with this organization. It's worth looking at.

Toastmasters (www.toastmasters.org)—This is a good group of people and I have lifelong friends and networking partners from my twenty-plus years of being around the organization. So, go get neck-deep involved with Toastmasters.

> Some of us learn from other people's mistakes and the rest of us have to be other people.
>
> —Zig Ziglar

What I Wish I Had Known Before I Started My Business

Mike Phillips
Autogeek.net
Stuart, FL

Find a seasoned professional and become his or her apprentice. I wish I would have known and understood the value of finding a mentor, someone older than me with an impeccable reputation for doing top-quality work, who would share with me the lessons they had spent a lifetime learning. The most important part of being successful is learning the business side of the car-detailing industry. Instead of learning through trial and error like so many of us did, a faster road to success would be to learn firsthand from someone who already has a time-proven record of success. One of my favorite quotes is from Eleanor Roosevelt and it goes like this: "Learn from the mistakes of others. You can't live long enough to make them all yourself."

Join a detailing discussion forum. The one thing that people have today that I didn't have when I started out is the Internet. The Internet empowers you like nothing else and dollar for dollar, it's the best bang for the buck whether you're educating yourself on the business or work side of the industry or marketing yourself. I've had the blessing of moderating and working on two of the most popular detailing discussion forums on the Internet, www.MeguiarsOnline.com, which I brought up from scratch in 2004 for Meguiar's; and www.AutogeekOnline.net, which I work on for Autogeek.net.

Discussion forums are powerful because you have access to available information as it is generated. Discussion forums are where you learn about all of the newest products, tools, and emerging technology before they are even introduced to the marketplace. Detailers who hang out on quality detailing discussion forums ALWAYS know more than detailers that don't. Always.

Besides learning about products, tools, and technology, you can also learn techniques from experienced and seasoned professionals. A good forum attracts high-caliber people who enjoy helping others to be successful—that's what attracted me to discussion forums when they were first introduced around 2000. They eventually led me to a full-time job simply answering how-to questions for others and sharing articles, pictures, and videos.

If you're reading this and thinking about getting into the detailing business in any of its dimensions, whether it's production detailing, show car detailing, boat detailing, or even airplane detailing, find a friendly, professional detailing discussion forum and start reading. After you've soaked up a ton of information, join in the fun and start participating in the forum by asking questions and getting feedback from others.

The philosophy I practice when working on discussion forums is one I learned from Zig Ziglar: "You can have everything in life that you want if you will just help enough other people get what they want."

Every quality discussion forum has a hard-core group of detailers that practice this philosophy whether they know it or not. So do some surfing, find a forum you feel comfortable with, and start reading and asking questions. In due time, you'll be helping others too.

Detailing Diary

Based on conversations I have had with over 150 professional detailers before they obtained training, here is a common diary that will give you a true look at what you could be facing if you are not detailing educated:

December 6: It's hard to believe I started my detailing business over six months ago. I am working long hours trying to build my business and while in the beginning my friends and family provided me with leads, business has slowed. I am looking to start some new marketing efforts following the holidays but all these ads I am taking out are expensive. I sure hope it all works!

January 3: I took out ads in two local magazines and sent out over 5,000 postcards, and all that effort did little for my business so far. In the beginning, my friends and family really supported my new business with some great cars to detail, and things were great. My opening efforts with marketing my detailing services did not go over as well as planned. I am meeting with the Yellow Pages rep in a couple days. When the new book comes out I am sure I will get very busy!

February 13: While I think the work I am doing is good, I am still intimidated by high-speed buffer paint correction. While I watched a few online videos and read all I could on the web, my paint correction is missing something.

February 27: I think I am taking way too much time within the details I am performing. I am working on some cars six, seven, or even eight hours. Does it really take this long? It can't. How are others making money detailing? I need to find someone who is making money in the detailing business and pick his or her brain!

March 23: My Yellow Pages ad came out nearly four weeks ago. I was so excited. I knew it would be busy when that ad hit, but business remains slow even with the ad.

March 24: It seems I am either really busy or really slow. At times I cannot keep up with the workload and then all of a sudden I am slow again. I am going to spend more money on marketing and see if that helps.

April 1: I worked eight hours on one car today. How am I going to make any real profits if it's taking me that long to detail one single car? After months and months I am spending a lot of time on the cars I detail and I am not making near enough profits from my efforts.

April 13: When I started the business, I really was hoping I could be doing two details a day by now but I am lucky to be doing one. I hope my marketing kicks in soon.

April 18: I received a call today to work on a really nice car and I should be really happy about it, but I am scared to death. I am really confused and not sure if the work I am doing is effective and safe. To add to my worries, I am really slow and my Yellow Pages ad has generated minimal calls.

April 20: I spent over $3,000 on my Yellow Pages ad and so far it's not performing like I guessed it would. Looks like I will need to find additional marketing ideas.

April 29: I am going to start looking around the web and see what else I can learn about detailing. I looked all over before I started but I really felt it would be easy to succeed and now that is proving to not be so true. Did I make a mistake?

May 5: I found several sites on detailing the last couple weeks. I found a site that is killer. This guy has detailed everything under the sun, even multimillion dollar private jets. He sounds and looks like he is a true Master Detailer that trains others like me on the proper use of high-speed buffers and other important skills needed within detailing. I e-mailed him tonight to find out more on his trainings.

May 10: I have received a ton of information from detail training facilities. Some are schools but I keep going back to the one that offers private one-on-one training and I like the idea of not sharing my training time with others. The others I have spoke with offer group trainings (4 to 20 people) and it seems that I would have very little hands-on time. The trainers I prefer have been very helpful when I spoke with them. The private training opportunity is really standing out. I would be the only student this guy works with and the website states, he has been there, done that in the detailing industry.

May 14: I spoke with three detail trainers the past couple days. While I enjoyed speaking to them all, I have more research to do on possibly attending detail training.

May 16: I spoke with four training organizations—the differences are huge! I was shocked to hear two explain that they do not "prefer" to train on high-speed polishing as they don't see the need. From what I read that's not what the true pros of the industry say. The other options seemed more like a school and not detailer based. I think I would rather learn from someone who understands my day-to-day struggles and is not simply hoping to sell me a bunch of equipment and products.

June 3: I start training this morning and I am excited to learn a new way of detailing. We will spend the first day discussing the marketing and sales approaches that work in the detailing industry. I am very excited to learn about these approaches and see how they use proven marketing methods to gain high referral numbers and customer retention.

June 13: All I can say is WOW! I have been back home for just over a week after spending five days training and what I learned is already paying off! My timing is far better and my profits per hour have increased.

What is even better, I have already doubled the number of referrals I gain from my detailing clients. I am so excited to already be realizing a return on my detail training investment!

I also performed my first Signature-level detail yesterday and was amazed with the outcome! My client was shocked at how good his black vehicle looked and I was amazed at how easy high-speed polishing is.

June 25: I started to use what I learned about my approach to sales and profits. I went out today and performed several detailing demonstrations and sales calls with organizations that my trainer highlighted as being detailing-friendly targets. I was asked to provide a proposal by one organization and my detailing coaches assisted me with pricing, writing, and presenting my proposal!

July 3: I got it! My first major account! This one account will be worth $10,000 a year. I also have a couple of other new accounts and the good news is that the cost related with finding these new clients was very low due to all the networking, marketing, and sales skills I learned.

December 24: I can't believe it. My business has nearly doubled since my training back in June and I sold over $2,000 worth of gift certificates this Christmas season. I am so pleased. My life is on the right course now and my stress level has been greatly reduced. The training path I chose was the right one.

One year following training: I never dreamed that I would be landing accounts like I am. The new menu my trainer helped me design last year is doing exactly what it was meant to do—sell more services! I am offering services ranging from express details to show-car finishes, and making a profit thanks to my expert trainers. To my detail coach, thank you! Detail training changed my detailing abilities. Your coaching changed my life! I recently expanded my business and I am looking at starting another business piggybacked off my detailing business. I would have never guessed my detailing business would be the foundation for this type of lifestyle.

Do you have a true passion for cars?	Y/ N ☐ ☐
Do you enjoy detailing your own car?	Y/ N ☐ ☐
Are you able to obtain professional-level results within your detailing efforts now using professional grade detailing tools?	Y/ N ☐ ☐
Do you tend to be extremely picky about cleanliness?	Y/ N ☐ ☐
Do you have a contagious personality? (A real people person)	Y/ N ☐ ☐
Do you have an eye for good paint versus nasty, swirled paint?	Y/ N ☐ ☐
Do you have the drive and energy to work harder than you have ever worked for the three to five years it will take to get your new business on solid ground?	Y/ N ☐ ☐
Are you comfortable selling services and thus communicating with people both on the phone and in person?	Y/ N ☐ ☐
Are you comfortable using common household tools? (You do not need to be a tool jockey or a Mr. "I Can Fix Anything." You simply need to be comfortable around tools. The rest can be learned.)	Y/ N ☐ ☐
Can you adapt and learn new technical and social skills? (If you are not a people person and really do not care to become a people person the answer is no)	Y/ N ☐ ☐

If you answered eight of the above questions with a yes, you could be a Detail Warrior!

If you answered seven of the above questions with a yes, you have what it takes, in most cases.

If you answered less than six of the above with a yes, you need to dig deep and ask yourself if you are right for detailing or if detailing is right for you.

What I Wish I Had Known Before I Started My Business

Mike Rafael and Tom Shearer
Mr. Detail
Seattle, WA

The year 2009 was when we took Mr. Detail Auto Salon to the next level. When Mike and I started, we used the knowledge we had from working on our own cars and the techniques we picked up online in forums and videos. We wanted to produce a superior product, and we knew if we wanted to be the "big dog in town," we needed to get trained and certified somewhere.

We didn't pay ourselves that whole year in 2008, given we didn't make a ton of money; we knew we needed to save to upgrade our business image. I started shopping online for auto detail training schools. I wasn't able to find many schools, probably three that sparked an interest. Now came decision time, where do we go? We decided to train with Renny Doyle of Attention to Details. It proved to be the best decision we've made thus far. Training with Renny not only gave us the knowledge we needed to produce that superior product, but extreme hands-on training to go home and be comfortable using tools and products we hadn't used before. Good-bye hand polishing, hello Flex DA.

Going into our fourth year of business, the team we are involved with and the networking we do together is something we never saw in the beginning yet is something we now can't see without.

Mike and I have landed two fixed locations in the heart of Downtown Seattle, one in the Columbia Tower, a massive seventy-eight-story business complex. We knew with the rainy season here in Seattle, we needed a shop and we were lucky enough get the facility in the Tower just three months after training. It was a crazy time, things just started happening for us, and it really felt like we were taking off and that our name was getting out.

We still wanted to have a mobile service and knew that our little trailer didn't fit our image or the company we were trying to become. We went out and purchased a 2010 Transit Connect along with a blueprint from Renny on how to set up a mobile unit. We now have a state-of-the-art mobile department. And with a full vehicle wrap on the side, we are a rolling billboard.

Looking back on everything, I wish that we had been trained and certified before launching our company. I wish I could go back to every client's car that I worked on prior to being trained and do the car over again with all the tools and knowledge that I have now. That's business though. You learn as you go, and it all makes you stronger and better in the long run. We are fortunate enough to have loyal clients who have been coming to us from the beginning and witnessed our growth first hand, not only as a company but as individuals.

Within my first businesses I made several near-fatal errors, errors that all too many young entrepreneurs make. I tried to be everything to everybody. I wanted to offer every level of service and create every profit center I could think of.

To make things worse I truly did not understand what my prospective customers truly desired.

Twenty years later I have a solid understanding of my chief reasons for being in business—my lifestyle, my family's financial health, and my passion for cars, airplanes, and bikes.

Owning a detailing business is, for many of us, an addiction to shine. The shine of a car is a huge turn-on and we strive for perfection. For some, that perfection is a road to success, for others it will prove deadly to their business.

Establishing a Loyal Customer Base

Do you consider the fast-food way of thinking when looking at your detailing business? The tie-in between detailing and fast food is the notion of customer loyalty.

Let's start with the In-N-Out Burger way of thinking. If you have never been out west, In-N-Out Burger may not be a familiar name to you, but here in California, Arizona, and Nevada, the In-N-Out name is unequaled by any other fast-food chain. It has a loyal following equal to Harley Davidson out here. In-N-Out has created a loyal customer base that is near cultish and they deserve it. If my family or I are in the mood for a burger and fries, it's off to In-N-Out we go! We are loyal, and in my detailing business, I have used the In-N-Out model for nearly two decades.

Loyalty within detailing starts with that first phone conversation with a prospective customer or the first visit they make to your shop. Another first impression is how your mobile detailing unit looks. First impressions are vitally important. Prospective customers need to walk away from their first encounter being impressed with your knowledge and overall offer.

The next important step is the first detail service you provide. Call customers the day before to kindly remind them of the appointment, and don't you dare be late. Also keep your mobile work area clean as you work and when you finish, the customer should not be able to tell you were even there. Your work quality needs to be exactly what you sold them, and meeting or beating their expectations is important.

I love it when I watch some of those I coach interact with their customers. Seeing them present the vehicle, explaining what was done with the car, why it was done, and what they could not accomplish and why. They connect with their new client and really start to educate them, sharing the details of their work.

This next step is a lost art today, the handshake and request that the client share your name and services with others they know. I shake hands with everyone I do business with (as long as they are not protesting the action) and while doing so, I politely ask them to share our services with their family, friends, and coworkers. This is a major step.

Selling to Your Market

Always detail at your customer's desired level of spending. As a younger detailing professional, I misunderstood profits. I was often giving my clients hours of no-profit services. I would over-deliver and undersell many jobs and our profits were not what they should have been.

Realizing that, I developed an easy-to-use, write-in hourly profits tracking form. I soon started to see my exact profits and thus, my eyes were opened to my hourly performance. I made adjustments and developed systems to help me be more profitable.

Do you know what your exact costs are? Do you understand your profit level? If you said yes, congratulations. You are within a small group of professionals. If you said no, you better change your ways. Tracking your profits is important, and I have included a sample of the form I have used for many years. It is an uncomplicated form that is very easy to use, and very helpful for your business. Of all the tracking I have done within my detailing business, the tracking of my profits per hour was one of the most important steps I have taken.

What I Wish I Had Known Before I Started My Business

Joe Fernandez
Superior Shine Mobile Auto Detailing
Arcadia, CA

I wish I had understood my ideal customer when I started my business. At one time, I thought everybody who owned a car was my potential client. Over the years, I have learned that it is certainly not the case. In other words, I wasted countless hours trying to sell steak to vegetarians, and ice cream to health nuts.

I can get a vehicle finish perfect. It is labor-intensive work and a premium must be charged in order to be profitable. One year, I put together a postcard campaign touting how nice we could a get vehicle's paint to shine. I had 5,000 postcards sent out five times over a three-month period to the same 5,000 addresses in a middle-income area. So here are these soccer moms and dads who were in predominantly blue-collar fields getting a mailer saying we could get their paint perfect for $500. The campaign failed horribly. I didn't match the service with their needs.

A decision will need to be made about who your target market will be. That market must want and/or need your services, and have the resources to pay for them. You will need to match your services according to their needs. What problems do you solve and who needs them solved?

Another postcard mailer I did was very successful. I selected a very small, affluent area. I told them that I was a small, reliable, and convenient service that did high-quality work. Out of the fifty mailers, I landed two clients. I currently earn approximately $20,000 a year from those two clients combined.

Over the years I have dabbled with various target markets and at times completely dropped one group for another. You need to fine-tune who your market is, keeping in mind that the most profitable may not be who you expected it to be. Home in on your ideal customer, meet their needs, and rake in the cash.

Designing Your Menu

Your customers are looking to you to be the expert. Design a menu that benefits both you and your clients. Keep your menu simple and be able to mix services easily. We sell signature interiors with express exteriors all the time. We mix and match any and all of our services, as long as the car matches that need. We will not perform a lesser-level detail only to save a person money while possibly damaging our reputation. I will refuse a job if that client is not willing to spend the money needed to bring their automobile up to the level our reputation deserves.

Express Detail

I learned about the express detail from entering cars into classic-car shows in Southern California back in the late '80s and '90s. We cleaned our cars before we left for the show, then again after we arrived. No trailer babies for us, we drove our cars. We took the techniques we learned from car shows and twisted them a tad into a retail-level service designed with the well-maintained automobile in mind.

The express detail allows the detail professional to offer, and the customer to buy, a great service. This is an affordable service for people who desire both regular service and a clean car.

When we first started offering express detail, we worried that many of our clients would flip from their two or three deluxe- or signature-level details a year to express-level details. It did happen with our most finicky clients, but those same clients went from spending an average of $800 a year to over $1,100 a year. We were jazzed to

Are you addicted to shine? Ask yourself these questions:

1. Do I spend too much time on making the paint perfect on detail jobs under $300?
2. Do I add in additional paint correction steps even if the customer is not paying for that extra service?
3. Do I "have to" make the paint as perfect as possible on every job?

If you answered yes to any of the above, you may have PPD (Paint Perfection Disease). To cure this condition, follow these steps:

1. Track your man-hours on each job. Know and understand your per-hour performance.
2. Design a menu that allows your customers to pick out a detailing service that matches their pocketbook.
3. Upsell your services. When the customer needs more paint correction or interior work, don't give them the add-ons, sell them the add-ons. More on this to come in the next chapter.
4. Understand that express-level detailing can be as or even more profitable in many parts of the world as show-car level detailing.

All details are not created equal. You can have car after car come to you for a detail and treat them all the same for the exact same price. It's not the fact that you may go broke, it's the fact that you WILL go broke. For decades, the detailing industry has fallen victim to the one-price-gets-all mentality, and that mindset has sunk more detailing businesses than it helped. If you put yourself in that trap, you are in trouble. Sell from an effective menu designed from sound research and stand out from the herd. Don't be part of that boring, barely-making-it herd of losers. Take a look at the "Sample Detailing Menu" on page 113 for a quick overview and then we'll go into greater explanation on each level.

Express Detail	Deluxe Detail	Signature Detail	Show-Car Finish Detail
Wash Exterior	Wash Exterior	Wash Exterior	Wash Exterior
Dress Tires	Dress Tires	Clean Engine	Clean Engine
Apply Wax	Treat Wheel Wells	Measure Paint and Clear	Measure Paint and Clear Thickness
Clean Windows	Clay Exterior Low-Speed	Thickness	Microscope Inspect Paint Defects
Vacuum Interior	Paint Polishing	Microscope Inspect Paint	Deep Clean Paint
Clean Dash	Apply Advance Paint	Defects	Clay Exterior
Wipe Door Panels	Sealer	Deep Clean Paint	Wet Sand*
Clean Cup Holders*	Clean Wheels	Clay Exterior	6-8-Step Paint Correction*
Dress Interior	Clean Mirrors	Spot Wet Sand	Apply Paint Enhancer (wax)
Clean and Condition	Clean Windows	2-3-Step Paint Correction*	Dress Tires
Leather	Vacuum Interior	Apply Paint Sealer	Clean Wheel Wells
Clean Windows	Clean Dash Surfaces	Apply Paint Enhancer (wax)	Treat Wheel Wells
Final Inspection	Clean Nooks and Cran-	Dress Tires	Clean and Polish Wheels*
	nies	Clean Wheel Wells	Apply Wheel Seal
	Wipe and Clean Door	Treat Wheel Wells	Vacuum Interior
	Panels	Clean and Polish Wheels*	Q-Tip Clean All
	Clean Cup Holders*	Vacuum Interior	Nooks and Crannies
	Dress Interior	Q-Tip Clean All Nooks and	Clean Dash
	Clean Carpets	Crannies	Deep Clean Door Panels
	(light)	Clean Dash	Clean Cup Holders*
	Clean Leather	Deep Clean Door Panels	Clean Seat Bases
	Condition Leather	Clean Cup Holders*	Deep Clean Carpets
	Clean Doorjambs	Clean Seat Bases	Apply Carpet Sealer
	Final Inspection	Deep Clean Carpets	Apply Interior Surface Protector
		Apply Interior Surface Pro-	Deep Clean Leather
		tector	Apply Leather Sealer
		Deep Clean Leather	Clean and Wax Doorjambs
		Condition Leather	Multi-Step Super Cleaning of All
		Clean and Wax Doorjambs	Glass and Mirrors
		Multi-Step Super Cleaning	Final Inspection
		of All Glass and Mirrors	
		Final Inspection	

*Subject to additional charges depending on condition

see people spending more on detailing services, and we were happy to see them on a more regular basis. Guess what else grew? The number of referrals we got from these express-detail clients.

An express detail has been designed to be fast while offering real value for the customer. Here is an overview of what it includes:

- Prep the exterior—I use a pre-cleaner to loosen the grime and allow my wash mitts to travel across the surface smoothly during the washing.
- Perform a nice wash—High-quality car shampoo and high-quality wash mitts are essential during the washing.
- Clean the wheels—This task is important. It's best to use an all-wheel-safe cleaner.
- Dress the tires—The wheels and tires on modern-day vehicles are focal points so you need to make them both pretty.
- Apply a sealer to the paint and exterior surfaces—Of all the steps on the exterior during the express-detail process, this is the most important. All eyes are on the paint and making the paint shine is key. Note that you will not usually have time to apply a sealer by hand on this level of detail, so finding a wet applied (applied to the vehicle while the vehicle is wet) or, my preferred method, a spray-on-and-wipe-in sealer. I look for products that create intense shine, offer solid durability, and flow onto all exterior surfaces, including the glass, without smearing.
- Clean those windows—Think about this: when your detailing clients are driving around in their clean vehicles, what are they looking at the most or, should I say, what are they looking through? The windows, right? You need to be very careful to get the glass spotless.
- Doorjambs—I hate to open a clean car's doors and see dirty doorjambs. Make certain to get the jambs.
- Don't forget the trim, chrome, and bumpers—Make sure to get all the little items too. Again, a good-quality sealer can reduce your workload by doing a good job on ALL exterior surfaces, but don't forget these exterior surfaces as they are important to detail as well. Just make it quick and easy by using the right products.
- The inside—you need to clean and dress the interior hard surfaces. We like to do both at once using a water-based dressing with a little cleaner mixed

in. This speeds up the process while giving a very nice look. The nice thing about water-based dressings is that you can adjust the amount of shine the dressing offers by adjusting the amount of product. I love Meguiar's Hyper Dressing for this exact purpose. I have used it for years and can't find anything better. I use it mixed 4:1 ratio with a little auto-detailing, all-purpose cleaner mixed in. This is a great mix to not only dress and clean the hard surfaces, it will also do a nice job of cleaning up the center console and cup holders, which are areas people expect to be clean.

- Clean and dress the leather—Again, look for a product that will perform both steps in one.
- Clean the glass (inside and out), the vanity mirrors, and the rearview and exterior mirrors.
- Finalize with a good vacuum—Again another biggy for this service.

The express detail does not include heavy cleaning, such as stain removal or the removal of dog hair or kid grime. Remember, this level of service is designed for the well-maintained vehicle. Express details should be completed within one to two man-hours. The express detail is not for every level of automobile. Dirty cars need not apply.

Deluxe Detail

This level offers the client a great value and is both affordable and easy to perform.

If you were to talk with every person in the USA who purchased detailing, you would find that the vast majority were buyers of deluxe-level details. Here's what it includes:

- Prep the exterior—I use a pre-cleaner to loosen the grime and allow my wash mitts to travel across the surface smoothly during the washing. This may also include removing bug splatter and other debris from the exterior surfaces.
- Perform a nice wash—Using a high-quality car shampoo and high-quality wash mitts are essential during the washing. Did you upsell an engine detail? This is a good time to perform that service if you did.
- Clean the wheels—Using an all-wheel-safe wheel cleaner.
- Clay the painted surfaces—Claying removes paint contamination, environmental fall out, and other materials from the paint surface. It should be performed every time you are going to apply a machine finish.

- Dress the tires.
- At this level of detail, a little paint correction could be expected but I want to stress that this is an entry-level detail. If the vehicle's paint just needs a little improvement, that is acceptable but if the vehicle is in need of serious improvement, you need to upsell the client to the next higher level of detail. Basically this level of detail will put a nice shine to the paint and add a layer of protection in the form of a sealer or wax. Many times manufacturers make a product called single step that polishes and adds protection in one easy step.
- Remove excess paint corrective leftovers—No one likes the white residue left behind in the cracks and name badges, so remove it with detail brushes or better yet, a detailing steamer. This is massively important at this level. It is at any level, but once you are detailing on this level, you'd better not leave wax behind.
- Dress exterior trim and plastics—Again we are stepping up our game and utilizing a superior dressing product or dye.
- Dress the wheel wells as this is a great finishing touch.
- Clean those windows.
- Doorjambs.
- Don't forget the trim, chrome, and bumpers.
- Start the interior of this level of detail with a good vacuuming.
- Clean all the vents, tight areas, cup holders, screw holes, and control panel areas.
- Clean, then dress the interior hard surfaces. Not all clients want dressing at this level, so ask them. Also, there are dressing and protectants, and at this level it's better to protect versus dress.
- Deep clean the leather and follow up with a quality leather conditioner.
- Stain removal at this level is at the moderate level meaning you are going after common stains such as coffee and dirt, but you should not be dealing with heavy stains on carpets or sport seating. Those levels need to move to the next higher level of detail.
- Clean the carpets following the stain removal steps.
- Clean the glass (inside and out), the vanity mirrors, and the rearview and exterior mirrors.
- Finalize with a good vacuum.

Start to finish, I can get this level of detail completed in two to four hours.

When we perform deluxe-level details we NEVER include high-speed paint correction. This level of detail simply does not allow both high-speed paint correction and profit. Another opportunity to upsell!

The simple fact is that if a professional detailer knows his/her art and they are using the right polishers, they can outperform a great number of detailers using high speed. We outperform with both knowledge and skill—and you can too.

Signature Detail

In most cases, when a "car guy" purchases a detail you have your work cut out for you. Why? Car guys and gals understand paint correction, swirls, and micro scratches, and they expect stains to be removed from the interior. They want a good-looking detail. But not all of them understand how time consuming paint correction is or, when done right, how a trashed interior can take twice as long as an exterior detail.

When a customer has serious issues such as paint defects, or they want their wheels polished and not just cleaned, and their interior has stains or odor issues, we sell them a signature-level detail. Here's what this level includes:

- We prep the exterior using a pre-cleaner to loosen the grime and allow high-quality wash mitts to travel across the surface smoothly during the washing. This may also include removing bug splatter and other debris from the exterior surfaces.

- Perform a nice wash—Using high-quality car shampoo and high-quality wash mitts are essential during the washing. Did you upsell an engine detail? This is a good time to perform that service if you did.
- Clean the wheels.
- Clay the painted surfaces.
- Dress the tires.
- At this level of detail, a fair amount of skill-based paint correction is expected. This will, in many cases, involve wet/dry sanding, compounding, polishing, and final finishing. All of these steps take skill and making a profit at this level is like walking a tight rope for many. They may be highly skilled and able to perform at this level but few charge and make the level of profits that this level of detail service demands. There are many times I will have twelve to fifteen hours into the paint of a job like this without blinking an eye.
- There can be no leftover compound, polish, or wax on this level of detail— NONE.
- Dress exterior trim and plastics. Again we are stepping up our game and utilizing a superior dressing product or dye.
- Dress the wheel wells as this is a great finishing touch.
- Clean those windows. Important!
- Doorjambs. At this level can you say *spotless?*
- Don't forget the trim, chrome, and bumpers. *Perfecto* is the word.
- Start the interior of this level of detail with a good vacuuming. I mean good.
- Clean all the vents, tight areas, cup holders, screw holes, and control panel areas.
- Clean, then dress the interior hard surfaces. Not all clients want dressing at this level, so ask them. Also, there are dressing and protectants, and at this level it's better to protect versus dress.
- Deep clean and exfoliate the leather, and follow up with a high-quality leather conditioner.
- Stain removal at this level can be very involved. Knowing your interior chemistry and which products to use are essential.
- Clean the carpets following the stain-removal steps.
- Clean the glass (inside and out), the vanity mirrors, the rearview and exterior mirrors, and every piece of interior trim with any level of reflection.

- Finalize with a good vacuum. I don't leave vacuum markings (lines left by the vacuuming process) as this level of client usually wants a finished-looking product that doesn't include funky patterns in the carpeting.

This detail will take me five to eight hours to complete. It's that involved.

Is the signature detail all inclusive? No, but this level of service does include enough profit to allow a much higher-level service.

Remember, you have add-on items for a reason. We can't do everything for a set price and expect to make a profit.

This is a hard-core, eat-you-up detail. I don't care where you are in this country, if you are not charging at least $500 for this level of detail, you are better off getting a minimum wage job as a greeter at your local big-box store. This level of detailing is not for the novice, nor is this level of detail easy to perform. You better know your stuff and charge accordingly.

Show-Car Finish Detail

Many call this level a concours-level detail but no matter what the name, this service is all about TRUE paint correction and perfection at the show-car level. This level of detailing is pure art when performed correctly. When it comes to true show-car finishing, be prepared. This level of service is not often called for and is demanded only by true automobile aficionados.

I have worked at some of the world's leading automobile and aircraft events and can tell you that even the purest of automobile aficionados desire this level of perfection, yet few will actually pay for it. Why?

Few understand the level of skill and experience it requires or the time it will take to perform this level of detail. Detailers worldwide talk and dream about this level of service, but in reality only a handful of them make a living from it. Concours service includes interior detailing but it's really the final outcome on the exterior that matters. A show-car finish detail includes:

- Gentle prep of the exterior using a pre-cleaner is a must to make certain you loosen the grime and allow the wash mitts to travel smoothly across the surface during the washing. This may also include removing bug splatter and other debris from the exterior surfaces.
- Perform a very in-depth wash.

- Clean the wheels. Some of the vehicles you may be working on at this level could have some aggressive brake systems and these brakes can offer up challenges to getting the wheels clean. Specialty wheel cleaners are common at this level.
- Clay the painted surfaces. This service is most commonly found to be purchased by those with very nice vehicles, many times at the collector level. I use very pliable clays at this level, taking care to not introduce imperfections from the claying process.
- Dress the tires. Even the tires are upgraded at this level. I apply a high-end tire dressing system that is dry to the touch. Tires need to look new without the look of having a dressing on them.
- The paint correction involved at this level is painstaking and highly skilled, and you better have nerves of steel. Knowing how to get a piano finish on automotive paints can take years to learn and the great majority of the detailing industry today does not have the skills. I have spent anywhere from twenty to two hundred man-hours on this level of detail and I can tell you, it's tedious and taxing work.
- There cannot be one grain of compound, polish, or wax left behind. Not one towel thread nor any evidence that you worked on this car. It needs to look as if it has just been taken off the production line. It needs to be that pure.

For those of us who do perform at this level, I must share with you that it's exhilarating to perform this much work on a single vehicle and watch your art transform it. Show-car and/or concours-level detailing is realized by so few detailers for two key reasons:

1. It not only takes a solid education but also years of practicing the art.
2. Few detailing customers demand this level of service or are willing to pay it. Only a handful of detailers worldwide make a living from this level of service and those who do have invested years in their own knowledge and practice.

Detailer Tip

Your business is not a hobby. It's your way of life. Remember to offer and sell the items your customer desires and they will keep coming back, helping you build a loyal customer base.

To Do It All Over Again

Rick Goldstein

Rick Goldstein founded WOLFSTEINS PRO SERIES in 1996 to exclusively manufacture and supply premier automobile manufacturers with the world's first cleaning and protection system for convertible tops. He is a past president and is currently on the board of directors of the International Detailing Association. He also founded RAGGTOPP Convertible Top Care Products.

If you are starting a detailing business, you have now joined the world of entrepreneurs. You are that rare breed that has befriended terror and uncertainty to make a dream come true.

Welcome to the Club of Terror. I have been a member of this club, and have known terror for close to fifteen years. You can be sure you didn't bargain on this when you started your detailing company and became an entrepreneur. You won't find any college course on the subject or any on-the-job training programs. I never wanted to talk about or admit to the fear of entrepreneurial terror when starting my business. As a result, it remains a deep dark secret unless you admit to it by talking to fellow entrepreneurs and fellow detailers. You are not alone, and by wanting to start a business all of us are risk takers. The rewards are worth it.

I had no idea what lay ahead when I started my first company in 1996. You have the fear of failure, excitement of owning your business, and riding the roller coaster of highs and lows until you get your first sale. My wife will always remember my first thirty days in business and listening for the telephone to ring.

If I had to do it over, I would have a strategic plan, not just a business plan, to define my business vision. Vision will always pull you towards the future. Where do I want to be at some point in the future, who are my customers, and what do they say about me and my business? Creating a one-year business plan to support that vision will help provide the answers. Not all strategies can be implemented each year and you will have to update your business plan on a yearly basis.

It's natural to fear the unknown bumps along the way when starting and running your detailing business. However, you must learn that you are not alone and you have a whole gang of fellow detailers out there with the same fear. Terror is going to be a factor in starting and managing your business. But the rewards are worth it.

Rule One: Do not take terror home with you and do not, under any circumstances, share terror with the people you love unless they are partners in your business.

Rule Two: Learn to deal with fear and terror. "He Who Fears Defeat Is Sure To Become Conquered."

Building Your Customized Detailing Menu

When it comes to building a detailing menu, I will date myself a tad—and maybe sound a bit elementary—but base your menu on the KISS system: Keep It Simple, Stupid! Here's how:

- Don't go with a ton of services. Keep it to a base of four services plus your a la carte items.
- Keep the name of your service simple to understand.
- Don't start with the cheapest item, people will see cheap first and go with it.
- If possible, design your menu electronically and share that with your clients on an iPad or tablet.
- Base your menu on your local market. If you are in a modest market filled with minivans, are you really going to offer a show-car detail?
- Think of your abilities and be truthful with yourself. Design your menu based on what your capabilities are. Never do harm to clients' cars all in the effort to learn detailing. That is bad business and unethical to boot.
- Know your costs and expenses before you establish your pricing. Knowing costs and expenses will help establish the pricing you need to structure your business.
- Never base prices on competitor's prices. You can use other detailers' pricing as a guide, but never simply copy their price structure.
- Develop your menu system where you can interchange services. Let's say your menu items are Detail 1, Detail 2, and Detail 3. You should be able to combine an exterior Detail 1 with an interior Detail 3. Some cars are really clean on the outside and wrecks on the inside and visa versa.
- If you print your menu in a brochure or on your website, don't include prices. It takes the salesmanship right out of your hands.

While thinking of what your menu will look like, also keep the extras in mind that you may need to address. As detailing professionals, we get some weird requests to clean and detail a wide range of random stuff. Think about what you will charge per hour (your shop rate) and also, the add-on services you may offer. See appendix B for a customized sample menu design.

08

Additional Services to Offer

Detailing has different services that you should be offering. A wash, wax, and interior cleaning are just the start. There are dozens of additional services you can offer to make more profits and attract additional customers. (By the way, check out sealants. They offer some benefits and most upcharge for sealants. Why not include them and justify your slightly higher price?)

The Value of the Upsell

Remember the fast-food way of thinking in your detailing business? There are still more tie-ins to fast food and upselling is one of them.

Would you like an apple pie and Coke with your detail today? The big stores know that bringing customers in and carefully upselling them with add-ons can double sales.

Before we jump into add-on services, let's talk about the value and way to perform the upsell. To upsell, your menu and sales script need to support it. (I hate the word "script" but you do need to have one ready.) Transparency is key in upselling, so never be caught with the obvious sell. Trust is very, very important in luxury businesses like detailing. Make sure your menu, printed or not, is laid out to support the upsell opportunity. The questions you ask and the statements you make all need to be conducive and not aggressive. Otherwise you could anger some customers and lose the majority of upsells you attempt.

Detailing Quicksand

The quickest way to anger your customer base is with the term "full detail." It is recklessly used in this industry and is a sure-fire way to crash and burn a detailing business. Look at the definition of *"full"—containing as much or as many as possible*. When you or your menu say full, the customer thinks that everything

To Do It All Over Again

Mike Phillips

Autogeek.net

Mike is the Director of Training at Autogeek.net. He shares his extensive detailing experience and thorough understanding of vehicle surface care with other hobbyists and professionals at Autogeek's Show Car Garage Detailing Classes, held several times a year at Autogeek's headquarters in Stuart, Florida.

Mike is also the host of Autogeek's detailing tip segments featured on the TV shows *Two Guys Garage, Motorhead Garage,* and *My Classic Car.* He also hosts Autogeek's detailing how-to videos, and he will be hosting Autogeek's *What's In The Garage?* on the FOX Sports Network. He has over 250 articles to his credit and he's constantly testing and reviewing products on AutogeekOnline.net. In November 2011, Mike published his first book in a series called *The Art of Detailing,* available in paperback, e-book, and audio-book formats.

Mike gained his extensive detailing knowledge through trial and error and his drive to find the very best detailing techniques and products. He has been detailing since the 1970s when he hand-rubbed a three-stage process on his 1948 Plymouth Coupe. What began as a hobby has turned into a lifelong passion. Today, Mike is one of the foremost experts on auto detailing and paint restoration. His expertise is in machine polishing to remove swirls and create a show-car finish, wet sanding, cutting and polishing, and restoring original and antique paint on classic, antique, and special interest cars.

He has taught countless detailing classes since 1988 and has been a guest speaker at numerous car-club events and car shows. Prior to working at Autogeek, Mike worked at Meguiar's as a sales rep/trainer for Oregon, Washington, and northern Idaho, training body-shop and dealership technicians in the use of Meguiar's professional detailing products. Later, he became the online administrator of www.MeguiarsOnline.com and instructor of Meguiar's detailing classes. In the fall of 2009, Mike made the move to Autogeek.net to take on the job of teaching detailing classes and spreading good car-care practices to detailing enthusiasts via the Internet and television.

See what Mike is working on by joining AutogeekOnline.net, liking him on Facebook, and by watching Autogeek's *What's in the Garage?*

The Learned Skill of Turning Down Work

One of the biggest mistakes I made when I first started out was not charging enough for my work. I was eager for more customers to the point where I wound up charging less than what I knew I wanted for the job. In hindsight, I should have stated my price for the job and if a potential client balked at the price, I should have graciously told them that if my services were out of the range of their budget, I understood and moved on to my next job. The problem with undercutting yourself is that you're establishing your price range in the market. Once you do that, it's hard to raise your prices. So my advice to anyone starting out in this business is to determine what you're worth, set your prices, and stick to them.

It's important to understand that it's not about the money; it's about your self-worth. When you work for less than you're worth, you'll find you that while you appreciate the money, you regret the time and energy invested in the project. This is especially true when you learn that while you might be out of some customers' price range, there are still plenty of customers in your price range. You just have to focus your resources on reaching your target market instead of the lower-budget market. When you have customers willing to pay your price, instead of regretting a job, you'll value both the job and the customer. More importantly, you'll take great satisfaction in the services you provide.

is included. This spells trouble for true pros. The full detail brings the chance of an upsell down to a minimum, and why would you do that?

Set up your sales and menu systems with care as we discussed in the last chapter and don't overpromise or underdeliver, both are slippery slopes that are difficult to get off of once you are on them.

Add-On Services

Here are some of the most common add-on services to think about. In most cases, all of them can be completed with the equipment you already possess as a pro detailer.

Scratch and Blemish Removal

Before I detail a car, the first thing I do is walk the car with my client. We review the condition together, and when I spot a blemish, I ask them if it's important to them that I attempt to remove it.

It's amazing how many people expect that you are going to get every blemish and scratch out in a $150 detail, and I am here to tell you that you will go broke trying. I upsell for blemish and scratch removal and my hourly rate increases with these services, as they are specialized. Getting known as a specialist is a key way to make more money.

The average detailer in the US has minimal skills to deal with truly challenging blemishes, and therefore the average detailer struggles to bring in real money. By comparison, the highly skilled detailing pro can upsell when these opportunities arise and be more profitable.

Stain Removal

This is one of my pet peeves for sure. The standard detail should include carpet cleaning, not stain removal. There is a difference between carpet-cleaning services and stain removal. When we sell a job over the phone we always ask about "kid grime, dog hair, or any heavy stains." If they reply no, I upsell when they get to the shop and I see that carpets are stained. (Note: People don't exactly tell the truth about the condition of their cars, so be prepared for dealing with this fact.)

Many times they will ask, "Well, is that not included?" I respond by saying, "No, if you remember, I asked about stains and you replied no to my question, so I gave you an estimate based on no stains." Many times they will ask, "Well, can't you just get it out anyway?" My response is, "For an additional charge, yes; if you do not wish to pay, you will have clean carpets with clean stains but some of the stains will be there. Do you wish to upgrade to stain removal?" Don't give your work away, it's a bad habit to get into.

> **Detailer Tip**
>
> I love upselling stain removal. If you are equipped correctly this is a very profitable service!

Headlight Restoration

This is a no-brainer: 10 to 20 percent of the vehicles you will be detailing will have bad headlights, and the profits in this service are incredible. Some states are even mandating fix-it tickets for bad headlights. The best thing is if you have a proper detailing system (this system includes: headlight stripper, various sanding papers, compounds, polishes, and a bottle of IPA alcohol with various three-inch polishing pads) in place you will need less than $200 in investment to perform at a very high level within this specialty service.

Odor Removal

Of all the cars I have ever detailed, at least a third of those cars had some level of odor. Some were downright nasty, while others were unpleasant. I have made good profits for treating interiors for odors and today, with the new systems like the European steam we talked about earlier, the profits are even higher since the time dedicated to these services is minimal while the processes have remained at the same levels.

Rock Chip Paint Repair

Can you say *easy money?* I love this service and you can buy a pro grade kit for as little as $40. You can also invest in a pro kit for about a grand and spend all the way up to $8,000 for a kit. Start small and work your way up.

Window Tinting

I have owned widow-tinting shops before and the profit is there for sure! But don't think auto tinting alone, the "flat glass" segment of tinting is very profitable. "Flat glass" includes residential and commercial installation of both tinted and safety films.

Paintless Dent Repair (PDR)

Paintless Dent Repair is a system where dents on panels, hoods, and doors can be removed without the need of body-shop level services. In the past, dents and dings were removed utilizing paint and body shops to repaint the affected area. Today, most light-to-moderate dents and dings can be removed without the need of repaint or expensive body work. This is a skill-based service that takes a special breed to master. It is not for everyone but it is a very profitable service.

Bumper Scuff Repair

I call this my guaranteed $80-an-hour service. If you are in the right market and can attract the right customer base, you will make a solid profit from this service. The skills are specialized and to gain a reputation you will need training.

Clear Bra Application

Not for every market. There is an investment in both training and equipment, but there is money to be made if you are good at installing the clear bra, and in the right market.

Interior Repair

Almost daily I see interiors that need various repairs for burns, rips, and discoloration on leathers, cloth upholstery, and carpets. These repairs are outside of our scope of work but the skills can be learned and mastered with training and an investment in the needed tooling.

Windshield Repair

One word: saturated. There are window-repair companies all over the place and the prices of window repair are down in many markets. But on the flip side, if you have good relations with your customers, you could win some business. Another couple of good points about this service are the low investment it takes and the fact that the learning curve is not extensive.

Convertible Top Services

Two words: easy sell. All you need to do this service is stock the product and sell it. Check out the products available from companies like RAGGTOPP. Rick and his gang at RAGGTOPP make profiting from soft-top services easy!

Wheel Repair

Wheel repair is a unique service, and a highly trained technician can take a factory or custom wheel damaged with scuffs and abrasions and make it new or near-new again. This service involves reshaping the wheel edges, then recoating or repainting the wheel to match its original look. The equipment is expensive and you gotta be in the right market to make it pay.

Specialty Services to Increase Profits and Customer Base

Auto detailing is just one segment in the detailing industry and there are subcategories we can offer that are not directly related to detailing, even though the customer base is the same. Think about compounding your customer base (see chapter 10) and you will flourish.

Boat Detailing

The foundation of skills for automotive detailing can also be used in the marine segment of the industry, but you will need to sharpen your skills in paint systems as most marine-based vehicles differ from automobiles. Also, there is an array of surfaces that you will need to get familiar with. Boat detailing has a massive spread on the type of watercraft serviced. Here are some of the categories:

- Family sport/ski boats—Straight forward and not too difficult to adapt to changes in the materials used, but there is an adjustment.
- Pontoon boats—Yikes, these boats can be a real challenge and headache. The mix of aluminum and water and the fact that these boat owners usually tend to hammer these boats. I mean, the aluminum can be beaten to death and it will usually take a pretty harsh correction system to bring it back. Also, these boats have a huge "family" area that is usually torn up pretty bad. This level of boat takes a higher degree of skill and you better know how to price these services. Note: Today, there is big money in polishing the pontoons on these boats out to a mirror. It's a ton of work, but some wealthy boaters love to be different and some are willing to pay for that bling.
- Yachts—This is a very specialized level of service and you need to be very skilled in all areas of detailing. Some of these boats are the size of ships and the materials used in construction can be very exotic and therefore it takes special actions to care for the surfaces. If you tackle a large boat like this, you better be prepared!

Aircraft Detailing

Aircraft detailing is dear to my heart and what drove me to detailing in the first place. I love aircraft and have been around them most of my life.

While I am skilled and known for my work within the automobile-detailing arena, aircraft detailing has offered some of the highest rewards, both professionally and monetarily.

I have massive amounts of time and capital involved in my aviation-based career and it took years to build my abilities and reputation. The aviation community is small and well connected and you have but one opportunity to make it right. Bad service or poor quality will spread like wildfire and end you before you get started.

If you jump into this segment of the industry, do it by being educated and knowing it will take time to build your reputation and success.

Before we jump into the skills needed with aviation detailing, let's talk about reality and allow me to share some facts about myself and my experiences.

I fly, have been involved in search-and-rescue operations, and been in, jumped out of, and maintained aircraft. I tell you this as a way to gauge my level of awareness and education when it comes to aircraft. If you are going to venture into this segment of detailing, you'd better do your homework. Aircraft detailing the wrong way can kill people. If you think I am joking, here is a story from a major newspaper reporting an accident that occurred in the '90s:

> *Adhesive tape mistakenly left covering altitude and speed sensors caused the air crash in October of a Boeing 757 airliner that killed all 70 on board, Peru's Transport Ministry said late Friday.*
>
> *According to the evidence that has been found, it has been concluded that staff cleaning the lower part of the aircraft did not remove protective adhesive tape when they finished their work and so the sensors remained obstructed, a report of a special commission set up by the Transport Ministry stated.*
>
> *The report said the obstruction of these instruments explained the erroneous and confused information about height and speed of the aircraft.*

Aircraft detailing is a serious business. Expectations are high, the investment is significant, and the needed talents are massive. Let's talk about the segments found within the aviation marketplace:

- General Aviation (GA)—The GA aviation market is massive and contains small-to-mid-sized aircraft. Most people are familiar with the Cessna, which is a small, single-engine plane. The safety aspects of GA detailing are a massive concern but also, the materials and paint systems found on aircraft are a far cry from those in the automotive industry.

■ Corporate Aircraft—Like yacht detailing in the boat industry, this is a very specialized level of service and you need to be very skilled in all areas of detailing.

There are many, many safety concerns with this level of aircraft and again, the size of these planes can be massive with thousands of square feet of surface area to handle. The materials used in construction both on the exterior and within the interior can be very exotic and therefore take special actions to care for the surfaces. Before you go this direction, you need to have a tremendous amount of skill, knowledge, and know-how around aircraft.

RV Detailing

RV detailing does have its specialties and conditions that will test your abilities. The surfaces are various levels of fiberglass with the paint systems varying greatly from the entry level RVs to the high-end coaches.

The entry-level finishes don't hold up well and can easily be damaged while the high-end finishes are much higher quality. RV owners are perfectionists and, for good reason, have a very high expectation. Some of these land yachts can cost well over a million dollars. RV detailing can be very lucrative but you will earn every dime as this is not simple work.

Motorcycle Detailing

Before some of you reading this get your panties in a bunch, I am a lifetime rider and love bikes. Motorcycle detailing is the least-profitable segment of detailing. Most bike owners do their own work and when they have a detail performed, they expect the works, for pennies.

The menu for bike detailing is very simple and does not reflect our auto detailing menu at all. Bike detailing is tedious and extremely time consuming, so we keep the bike menu very pointed at what we have found to be both profitable and acceptable

To Do It All Over Again

Angelo Massaro
Precision Auto Detail, Inc.
Buffalo, NY

My love for cars came at a very young age. My older brother Dave was in the used car business and I was always fascinated by the cool cars that he would bring home. So when he asked me to wash cars at his car lot, I naturally said yes! I couldn't believe I was getting paid to wash all of these sweet cars. I didn't tell him at the time, but I would have done it for free. I also didn't know at the time that I would be doing this as a career later in life. I had always wanted to own my own business someday, I just didn't know what kind. I was asked by my brother if I wanted to detail cars at a new lot that he was building by a used car auction. He would buy and sell the cars and I would detail them. When I got my first car, I would spend hours on the front lawn meticulously cleaning it on a weekly basis. I enjoyed the time I spent cleaning my car and took pride in its appearance, so doing the same to other cars seemed like something I would enjoy doing on a daily basis. So that is where it all began.

My brother had showed me the basics and from there I began to master the art of detailing. Like most starting out in the business, I had minimal equipment consisting of a variety of brushes, a bucket, various chemicals, a wet/dry vacuum, and a buffer, which seemed to weigh 100 pounds. Through a lot of trial and error, my detailing skills began to improve and I became more efficient. I had seen a need for good quality auto detailing amongst the local dealers in the area and was now confident enough to offer my services to them. I had started out slow, with only one account, as that was all I could handle by myself. As demand grew, I hired my first employee and gained another account. As word got out about the quality of my details, I began receiving calls from other dealers regarding my services. So I hired more employees to keep up with the workload, eventually outgrowing my shop and relocating to a bigger shop with a more central location. I then began attending various trade shows with hopes of learning all I could about auto detailing, not only the technical side but the business side as well. With the confidence and knowledge I gained over the years, I then began to offer my services to the general public as well. After about four and a half years at that location, I was now ready to expand even more. So in 2004, after many years of hard work and determination, I was in a position to purchase my own shop, which is where I am now located and continue to prosper.

I wish I had known before I started my business the resources that are now available to us detailers. There are various professional organizations and forums available that I had no idea existed when I first started out. Also, find yourself a good training facility to hone your skills. I have attended a couple of different training schools over the years and the positive impact it has had on my business is priceless. I suggest to anyone starting out to research these resources and continue to educate yourself to become the very best detailer and successful business that you could possibly be.

to bike owners. We make the most of two services: our bike express detail and our basic detail. If a bike owner wants metal polishing, that is an off-the-menu item we sell purely based on the hours it will take to complete the task. I have detailed big street bikes and choppers that have taken me fifteen to thirty hours to complete. It's for that reason I really like to interview the bike owner first to find out what they really want. From my years around bike detailing, I have found that 50 percent of bike owners desire perfection at $150 and when you are going to spend fifteen to thirty hours on that perfection, there is no money in it. The remaining 50 percent just want a clean bike with a good coat of wax, which allows me to sell them a $150 detail and still make a profit. Again, bike detailing is tedious work and the man-hours can make you or break you. Make sure you have a nice conversation with the bike owner and find out exactly what his or her expectations are, then price the bike detail based off of those conversations.

Why Not Offer All of The Above Services, While NOT Actually Performing The Work?

There is a great saying that goes, "If you try to be everything to everyone, you'll be nothing to no one." I just gave you an enormous list of skills and services. To properly learn all the skills in ten lifetimes would be a challenge.

Instead, become a pro at detailing, add in all the easy-to-master services, and maybe one or two realistic skill sets like bumper repair and clear bra applications.

Better yet, network with those in your market and have them do their art on your customer's vehicles for you, and mark up their work. Subcontracting is huge in other industries and people profit from it all the time, but few within detailing take advantage of it.

Here is a list of subs I make money on by offering their services:

- Paintless Dent Repair (PDR)
- Wheel Repair
- Window Tinting
- Interior Repair
- Clear Bra Installations

I have used all of these in recent times and made a profit. For instance, I had my PDR guy do some work for a client. I was charged $300 for the work and was able to charge my client $425—not a bad return for making a phone call and selling my client on the service. I had about a half hour committed to the project. I will let you do the math on that return on investment.

Many say to think out of the box to succeed. I say, blow that box up! Capitalize on compounding your customer base and utilize the talents of others within your detailing business, and you can see levels and heights few see within our industry.

09

Web-Based Marketing

In 1997, my life changed forever. I got online for the first time and knew right then and there that this new media and resource would forever change my business. I knew I had a huge learning curve ahead as did the rest of the world. Today, the web is at the center of the most progressive detailing shops. The cutting-edge and profitable shops are mastering online marketing.

Web-based marketing is an art that is constantly changing. I like to compare the web to the western US during the 1800s. It's the new frontier with new opportunities popping up all the time. Keeping abreast of web marketing is tough, so stay connected and read a lot!

Believe me, I was a late bloomer when it comes to computers and the Internet, but over the past decade, I took it upon myself to change that fact and educate myself. Old and young dogs alike need to know and master the personal and technical sides of online marketing.

I won't say online marketing is more important than offline marketing, but I will say it's just as important over the long haul and a process you should pay attention to from day one.

With that said, let's dive into the online world of marketing your detailing business.

Five Key Online Sites for Website Building Templates

1. www.squarespace.com
2. www.wordpress.com
3. www.godaddy.com
4. www.facebook.com
5. www.detailingsuccess.com

Website Building and Management

Our first auto detailing site was built in the late '90s and consisted of five pages in total. It was basic at best and cost us nearly $2,000 to have someone build. Today, that site would be considered really, really basic and cost maybe $100 to build. In 2001, we built our second site, about twelve pages. It had flash headers and some really cool new technical advances, including a blog. Then in 2004, we had the site updated yet again and changed the domain to Detailing Success. The site was incredible and started what is my site today, but it had one flaw. I had to have a web designer make every change I wanted, and that got expensive.

In 2007, I decided that the site needed yet another overhaul and part of that overhaul included me having complete control of the site, including daily blog posts, and changes and additions. My buddy, Dan Ekenberg, the founder of Auto Detailing Network, was using Squarespace, a website template system, and loved it. Squarespace and Wordpress were both options, but after many long, late nights, I decided I would embark on building our next website on my own. It took me some four weeks and nearly 200 hours to build the site that you can see today.

I will be the first to admit that building our site was one of the toughest challenges of my career, but the rewards have been overwhelmingly positive. Within just a year, I was competing head to head with the big boys of detailing. Soon my ranks on Google and Yahoo were so successful, I had professional web designers asking, "How did you do that?" The new site catapulted me to my career as a detailing trainer, coach, and mentor. Since 2007, I have grown our site from some fifty pages to hundreds of pages, and saved tens of thousands not having to hire a professional web designer. I not only built our Detailing Success site, but also a handful of additional sites—including my own detailing services site—that are both useful and profitable. If I can do it, you can too.

I cannot stress enough the importance of a website. Furthermore, I am a believer that you really need to build your own site, or at least be able to manage the site yourself. The templates designed by Squarespace and Wordpress make building, managing, and profiting from your site a reality, even if you know nothing about website building or management. Here are a few things to consider when building and having a site built:

Choosing a Domain Name

You are most likely thinking of a domain name for your site, or maybe you already own one. Let me challenge rational thinking a little here. I surely am not a guru on the

> **Website Basics**
>
> 1. Your domain name is very important.
> 2. Have plenty of good content with keywords, including the areas you serve.
> 3. Update your site with fresh content on a regular basis.
> 4. Don't go with cheap, low-end templates. Use Squarespace or Wordpress.
> 5. Link up with local businesses with inbound and outbound links.
> 6. Sign up for Google Places and establish a Google Profile.
> 7. Make sure your metatags and keywords are dead on.
> 8. Make your site clean and professional. Have photos of you included on the site.
> 9. Make sure your phone number is easily found.
> 10. Use client testimonials. Video testimonials are best.

web, but I have had my own successes and I have worked with many detailing pros that have this web thing down. When it comes to choosing a domain name, there are common actions and assured actions that will help with your website's success. Your domain name selection is a very important step and you must keep an open mind. Don't get all cutesy with your domain, get creative and think ahead.

Most of us are going to be operating within a regional area, let's say Manhattan, New York. A smart detailing professional serving greater Manhattan will select a domain name such as manhattannydetailing.com or manhattannewyorkdetailer .com. If you build your site right, this will be a massive edge over your competitors and assist you with organic search results on search engines. In another example, let's say you are in Seattle, Washington, think about seattledetailing.com or maybe seattleautodetailing.com. Incorporating your regional area into the domain is very, very wise and search engines love practical domains that include something about what you do and where you are in the world.

My first domain was a copy of our company name and it proved to be too vague. Our site was being indexed by the search engines and mixed in with different services and industries not related to detailing. When we switched to Detailing Success, we worked our way into the leading spots within search engines and our profits soared.

If you are in a smaller market, such as Colton, California, I won't say that the right domain selection is not as important but it's not as critical. Colton, California, is my hometown and part of an area known as the Inland Empire. If I were to start a detailing business there, I would secure a domain like inlandempiredetailing.com or inlandempiredetailer.com. These domains would cover not only Colton, but also the towns and cites around it. Be picky about your domain name and perform some research of your own before you make the hard decision.

Keywords and Title Tags

When you are building, expanding, or adding to your website, including keywords with good content is very important. Some of the big search engines are looking for keywords and content as a primary tool for judging your website's value. Have words within your site that pertain to your business, your services, business within your local market, and your localized services.

For instance, I am located in Big Bear Lake, California, so my site needs to have the term "big bear lake california auto detailing" within the site. You also need to think about terms your prospective clients will search for. You may think "auto detailing big bear lake" while prospective clients are searching with the term "car detailing big bear lake ca."

Another fact is that your home page, usually the primary page of your site, needs to be rich in content related to your business. Your home page shouldn't be smothered with just pictures and videos. It should also have content that tells the visitor who you are, what your services are, and what you can do for them.

You need to include a wide range of terms on your site without being blunt or repetitive. If you get too repetitive your site will not be read correctly by visitors. Big search engines also consider overly repetitive content as misconduct, and they could simply make sure your site never appears on search engine results. To keep this from happening, I have a site blog that allows me to post content with key terms and

To Do It All Over Again

Mike Rafael and Tom Shearer
Mr. Detail
Seattle, WA

My name is Tom Shearer from Seattle, Washington. In early 2008 my best friend Michael Rafael and I had the idea of starting up a mobile detail company. We wanted to go mobile due to low start-up costs and there wasn't a ton of companies offering this service in our area. With an open market to tap into and our current network of family and friends, Mr. Detail Auto Salon was born in April 2008. If you can recall 2008, it was not an ideal time to start up a business. Our country was in the middle of a huge recession, jobs were disappearing, and money was tight. At the same time Mike and I were ready to leave our current jobs as valets, to do something we love, detail cars.

We did make wise moves, like trying our best to keep costs down as a start-up. The first thing we did was purchase our domain name, www .MrDetailSeattle.com.

Mike put the site together with a basic website template and it was so exciting to see our name and logo online. We put together a mobile unit, on an exposed trailer platform, which consisted of a 100-gallon water tank, generator, pump, and hose reel.

At the time that's all we needed. We placed all of our cleaning products in our black 1994 Jeep Cherokee that we used to tow the trailer and we had everything we needed to do the job anywhere. Our first job was a wash-and-wax package on a black Audi A4. I will never forget it. Looking back, it's crazy how much faster and efficient you get with the proper tools and training. That first 4-to-5-hour detail we did in '08 would now only take us 1.5 hours tops. Imagine the time we wasted. Getting the training, the mentoring, and a coach made a solid difference.

words within the blogs. Later within this chapter I will share some blogging input to make blogging easier and more understandable.

So let's talk about title tags. A title tag is a piece of meta-information required for all HTML/XHTML documents/sites. Think of the tag as the "title" of a web page, describing the overall theme of its content. Title tags can be of any length, but length and composition are greatly influenced by the fact that Google displays only the first sixty-five characters or so in search engine results. Each title tag on a website or blog should be unique, and completely relevant to the content of the page.

Aside from appearing in search engine results, title tags are displayed in other high-visibility locations, including in browser tabs and social media shares. Title tags can be one of the most important onsite factors for SEO (search engine optimization) because they tell search engines what each page is about.

Let me leave you with this note when it comes to content and tags: The online world changes fast and while my own success online has been very rewarding and I have assisted in building dozens of websites, you really need to do some research on your own or hire a true website professional.

Google Places

The best thing about Google Places is that it's free. Do a search in your local area for random businesses and services in your area and you will see varied Google Places pop up. You want your detailing business to be one of the businesses popping up when people perform random searches for detailing-related terms. For you mobile guys, Google Places can be tough because you have no physical address, and providing your home address is not advised as you don't want people randomly showing up at your home. You could network with another business and use that address as your physical address. There is a process, so visit the main Google Places website for all the details and facts on how to get your business listed.

Links

Links enable your website to be listed on another website or to have other websites listed on yours. Linking with local businesses is very important. Having both inbound (links from another site to yours) and outbound links (links from your site to another) are the key goal. I target other small businesses in my market and offer to link our site to theirs in return for a link on their site back to ours. This is mutually rewarding and usually a pretty easy task.

I also use my efforts on industry forums as a way to link back to my site with the posts I make. Most forums allow you to have a link to your business on your profile and this can be of big help in linking efforts.

Another good link is your local Chamber of Commerce. If you are a member, have them link to your site as a member and then link back to the chamber. (A great blog topic, by the way.)

Your social media efforts are also good links from you to various social media sites. Add in your link from YouTube and you have some great links!

Speaking of links, one of the most effective methods I have to linking is within my blogging efforts. Blogging has increased traffic to my websites by 15 to 30 percent this past year and blogging can enhance your linking efforts, all while driving traffic to your site!

Blogging

Do you remember the first time you heard the term "blogging?" I sure do and I was like, "What the hell is blogging?" Now, some ten years later, I am a blogger, at least when I am wearing my webmaster hat. Search engines like Google, Yahoo, and Bing are all looking for fresh content on your site and a blog is a great way to keep a steady stream of fresh, detailing-related content popping up. The most-asked question I hear about blogging is: "What do I blog about?" Remember, educating your marketplace is a primary mission so take the opportunity to educate people on the facts about detailing. Here is a short list to keep your blogging simple and start you out with your quest to blog on your detailing site!

Once you start blogging, it actually becomes easy and fun. Just be the car guy or gal you are and share your passion for the automobile.

Here are a few additional insights to blogging and the successes of a detailing blog:

- Make sure to spell-check (this is my weak link).
- Start by explaining what the reader is looking at. Basically, you want to become a good storyteller, so tell the story of your efforts or news.
- Include photos.
- Make video blog posts. The search engines love video on websites these days, especially Google.
- Make sure your blog (and website for that matter) is easy to read and the color combinations work.

Ten Examples of Possible Blog Posts

1. Blog about the difference between waxes and sealers.
2. Blog about a recent detail you performed and call out the city the car is from.
3. Blog about your use of steam within your detailing business.
4. Tell a story and share before-and-after photos of a paint correction you performed.
5. Share before-and-after photos of an interior detail you performed.
6. Blog about a local car show you attended.
7. Post a video and tell about a detail job. Make sure to include a verbal story about the project within the blog post. (Google loves video on your site.)
8. Blog about your different detailing packages (don't include the prices) and highlight each service in a new blog post.
9. Blog about a customer's business, and make them your customer of the month. (Add in a link to their site and ask them to link to yours.)
10. Post a blog about how to properly hand wash your car at home.

- Make two to five blog posts a week, every week, fifty-two weeks a year. That level of content will help you greatly within the page rankings of the search engines.
- Educate your client base. Take the time to share what separates you from the other detailers in the market.
- Once a month, make one of your clients a "customer of the month" and highlight that client and their local business. (I choose these customers of the month and try and play the connection game. Other business owners are worthy people to highlight on your blog as customers of the month, especially if they spend money with you.)
- Make sure your blog is part of your site. Some have their blog as a secondary site and I think this is a mistake.

I am not one who thinks you should show and share your prices online. When you list your prices, you take your salesmanship right out of the relationship. I am all about having your menu or services online, but I think instead of price, it should tell visitors to call for a free estimate. Each vehicle you detail is unique, and having a blanket price for all clients is the worst thing you could do for your sales efforts.

Social Media Marketing

When I first heard of social media, it was my kids telling me about this site called Facebook. So, I signed up for a personal account to keep track of my kids and guess what? Years later, social media is a huge part of my marketing efforts. There are so many types of social media that you need to think about as a detailer. Let's discuss the social media sites that will assist you at building your brand, your profits, and your detailing business!

Video Production and YouTube Realities

There is a saying that a photo is worth a thousand words and I think we can all agree with that. When we simply read something, it may be compelling but if there are key photos included, the impact is far greater, especially for those of us who are visual. Now, if a photo is worth a thousand words, a video must then be worth a million!

Video is not all that hard and it's cheap these days to get into. The days of really expensive equipment are long gone. Matter of fact, I know of people shooting video with their iPhone or Android-based cell phones and then editing it with the software that comes free with PCs and Macs. You can download Microsoft Movie Maker for free and iMovie for Mac is super cheap. I shoot my videos with a $200 camera and do all the editing on iMovie or Movie Maker.

I love before-and-after videos and you can add still shots into the video and make it pretty cool. The important elements within videos are clarity and sound followed by music. The music can make a detailing video. Make sure you use royalty-free music and images.

Royalty-free music is a term that refers to production music with no additional fees to pay after the music is bought. The music is purchased once and can be used again and again for a host of reasons. It is a much simpler way to make licensing music easier, cheaper, and more convenient. My favorite royalty-free music site is freemusicarchive.org.

Let me be clear: If you use a Jay-Z song in your detailing video, it's going to get you in trouble so don't go there. Also think about your prospective clients. Have the music on your videos be the type they listen to, not your style of music. Use music that is acceptable to a wide range of people.

Five Useful Video Tools and Sites

1. www.autodetailingtv.com—A detailing video site.
2. www.bmyers.com—A great video knowledge site.
3. www.vimeo.com—A video hosting site.
4. www.youtube.com/t/creators_corner.com—A how-to area on YouTube.
5. www.microsoft.com—Download Movie Maker for free.

Also, keep the video smooth and don't have your voice in the background saying, "Dude, that paint reflection is so sick, man." No one wants to hear you, they want to see the results. I like detailing videos that are one to three minutes in length and I like to see action, before-and-after pictures, and the results as soon as possible. Keep your audience engaged.

YouTube is the second largest search engine on the web. Video not only can connect you with clients or prospective clients, it can also assist you with finding new clients and for sure will assist you within getting your website ranked higher in your local market.

Facebook

If you are not on Facebook, you should be. Facebook is at the center of connective efforts with clients. Facebook is not a silver bullet for success but it should be part of your online marketing plan. You need get on Facebook and establish a business page. This will separate your business from your personal page. Your goal is to get others to follow you on Facebook.

I joined Facebook in 2009 and since that time, Facebook has doubled and now has over 750 million users. If that statistic doesn't drive you to be on Facebook, you need to go dig a hole and bury yourself. Social media–type sites like Facebook are not going anywhere, so get to it and join the rest of the world.

My mission on Facebook is following all the local businesses I can find and sharing between those links and page likes. Again, your local Chamber of Commerce may be a good source for you on Facebook and linking with them may get others following and liking your Facebook page. Also, go like my Facebook page, Detailing Success, and share your page with me, and I in turn will like yours! That's the simplicity of Facebook!

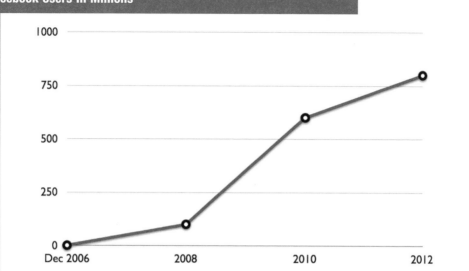

Facebook Users In Millions

Twitter

Ask.com explains Twitter best: "A free social networking website that lets users share short messages, known as 'tweets,' with their circle of friends." I am not a huge fan of Twitter but my sites do get traffic from the site. What I have done is set up my blog so that when I make a blog post, it automatically posts on Twitter. I use a system called www.hootsuite.com for this purpose and the best thing about Hootsuite is it's free!

Forums

Forums are both a love/hate thing with me. I know pro detailers who use the forums to market their services and some do very well. These people cruise various forums such as the Corvette, Ferrari, and other specialty-car brand forums, showcasing their detailing efforts and answering questions on detailing and automotive appearances. If you want to check out a few of these forums, here is a short list of those I keep a watchful eye on:

- www.benzworld.org/forums
- www.6speedonline.com/forums
- www.corvetteforum.com

Another variety is the detailing forums. Detailing forums range from the do-it-yourself market, to the serious enthusiast forum, to the pro-level forums. Today, most detailing forums are a mix of pro and pro-amateur level detailers. Visit the right forum for a wealth of information.

With that said, forums are the wild, wild west and people can say anything they like about detailing technologies, techniques, and products, and half of what you read is spot on. The other 50 percent of what you read can be viewed as hype. I have found that while there are great detailers taking part in these forums and sharing some impressive work, few are making a real profit in their detailing efforts. The guys making money in detailing are too dang busy to take part in forums at some point so you, the reader, are left with who knows what?

From my observations over the years, the forums I think offer true value are:

- Autogeek Forum (www.autogeekonline.net/forum/)—The forum is dedicated to detailing and rude, unprofessional posts are dealt with pretty quickly. Lots of great info about a huge range of products. A very nice forum for sure.
- Meguiar's Online (www.MeguiarsOnline.com)—Don't let the fact that this forum is directly associated with one of the biggest and most well-known detailing product manufacturers keep you from visiting this forum. Meguiar's Online is a well-run forum that covers more than just the Meguiar's line. I really enjoy visiting this forum due to the passion shared.
- Autopia (www.autopia.org)—This forum is very informative but can be a tad intimidating to the new detailer as they hold few punches and good, bad, and ugly posts can be found all over the site. Again, a good resource for cutting-edge info, just bring your thick skin along during your visits if you plan on posting.
- Auto Detailing Network Forum (www.autodetailingnetwork.com)—A forum that in the past has had the attention of the pro-level detailer but has slowed in recent years. The core site has a ton of information available.
- Auto Detailing Magazine (www.detailingmag.com)—This is a new start-up and a great source for detailing information laid out in a very unique format. The new magazine is dedicated to detailing and everything appearance-based for your car. The website has updates and detailing information.
- Auto Detailing TV (www.autodetailingtv.com)—This is a site that I am involved in. It reviews detailing products and equipment ranging from over-the-counter products to the elite boutique lines of detailing products. My

buddy Joe Fernandez co-hosts the shows with me and we have a ton of fun sharing with those who follow the show.

There are forums on every topic you can imagine and those I shared are a few I enjoy the most. Now let's dive into business promotional-related social media sites that can help you grow both your brand and your business.

Yelp

Detailing brothers and sisters, I am glad that I am well developed within the industry because I would hate to have to deal with some of the sites that new pro level detailers have to deal with during the early days of their business. Yelp is one of those sites I love to hate. While you can build your business by using sites like this, the freedom of others to post positive or negative comments is all too alluring to e-thugs and competitors who leave bogus claims. Yelp can be worth the effort but use Yelp knowing you will face ridicule and negative comments at some point, warranted or unwarranted, and the posts will be there for all to see.

www.Outbrain.com

If you build a nice blog-based website and start using Outbrain, you are going to want to kiss me in a few months for sharing this free tool with you. Here is a quick tutorial from its website on how Outbrain works:

"Outbrain automatically places your best content at the foot of your article to guide your readers toward more of what you have to offer.

"Our content recommendation system personalizes links for each of your readers. We blend contextual analysis, collaborative filtering ('people who read this article also read . . .'), and personalization to sift through all your content and select the best four or five links to show at any time. Outbrain also links to articles on other sites that partners are paying us to distribute. Like all our content recommendations, these paid links are targeted to provide your readers with the interesting content we think they will enjoy. In return, you share in the proceeds, developing a significant new revenue stream based on high user engagement that complements your editorial mission.

"As a result, your readers get a personalized data-driven selection of content they'll enjoy, increasing your traffic, your revenue, and your readers' loyalty, all in one step. No two readers are alike, so why should the content you recommend to them be the same?"

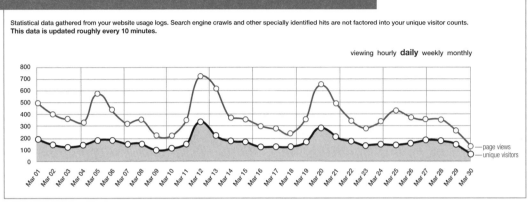

Outbrain is free, fully automated, and takes less than a minute to install. Above is a real-life sample of the web report from my own website. It shows that Outbrain brings over 16 percent of my total visitors weekly. When I get active with my blog-posting, Outbrain automatically posts my blog to more places across the web, which drives more traffic to my site. Can you see why I love this service?

Groupon and LivingSocial

Wow, how the world changes fast. It used to be coupons at the store or through the mail, now it's online coupons and mass marketing via sites like Groupon and Living-Social. Let me start by saying, if you are a mobile detailer or going to go mobile when you start your business, don't touch Groupon or LivingSocial. As a mobile detailer, you need to travel and that travel time when combined with the super-low profits made through Groupon or LivingSocial will cause you to go broke.

Most times, you are making an offer for services on Groupon or LivingSocial at a greatly reduced rate. Then, Groupon or LivingSocial will take up to 50 percent of the total sales. Ouch! This leaves you with very little money to cover expenses. Making a realistic profit is very, very doubtful and could drive you to the poor house. I want to share two possible offers that could work. I repeat, COULD.

The Entry-Level Detail: If you are in a moderate- to-mid-level market, the entry-level service may be the most sellable service to offer via a Groupon-style offer.

■ Exterior wash and wax

■ Wheel clean and wipe

■ Interior vac, wipe, and carpet/upholstery cleaning

- Dress tires
- Clean windows
- Wipe the doorjambs
- Final vacuum

The fine print: This service does not include items such as claying the car, debris removal from the exterior and/or debris, stain, or soil removal from the interior surfaces. Additional charges apply for moderate to heavily soiled exterior or interior surfaces. The removal of dog hair and/or sand particles is also not included and will be subject to additional charges. If you have any questions, please call us before making this purchase.

Bonus! We will throw in our air and surface purifying system that will kill the germs and bacteria that cause colds, flu, and other sicknesses. This is a $100 service! This is an easy service that takes almost no time to perform due to the fact that all you do is set your equipment into the car, turn it on, and let it do its thing!

Regular Price $325

Today's Deal $157 Over 50% off!

Limited to just 100 total coupons

The High-End Detail: My buddies Tom and Mike from Mr. Detail shared this idea with our group of pros (The Detailing Mafia). The idea is to give the market a higher end detail, with lots of add-on services such as odor removal and upgraded paint sealers. Both of these examples cost you, the business owner, very little in

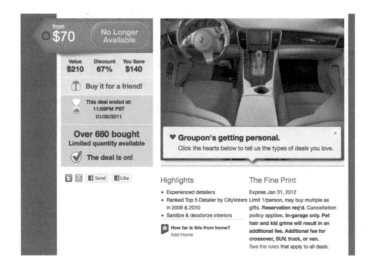

the form of labor, yet add value to the offer. Mike and Tom have done a great job of making the best of a social marketing offer. The offer is a high dollar amount in the area of four hundred to five hundred dollars, which, by the time the social media outlets take their 40 to 60 percent, still allows them to make a small profit on the campaign. This is a great offer to make during your slow period of the year and can be a fantastic avenue for building up your e-mail marketing list within the early stages of your business!

Making Your Groupon Offer Even Sweeter, and More Profitable

Remember that little "bonus" above? The odor killing system we use is a revolutionary, new, and environmentally friendly odor, germ, and allergen removal system for your customers' cars. Basically, it's a flu shot for your car and this service is easy to perform. It takes almost no labor, and adds value and much-needed profit to the deal. My buddies Mike and Tom offer this service and shared the concept with us. This idea was one of the best ways to increase your odds of making money with Groupon-style offers.

The Key to Groupon and LivingSocial Offers

Collect e-mail addresses for future marketing efforts and for your newsletter marketing.

Building Your Own Groupon-Style Offer

As you become more and more successful at gaining e-mail addresses, why not skip Groupon and build your own Groupon-style offer and keep all of the proceeds for yourself? Mark Johnson, a friend, fellow detailer, and car wash owner, shared this concept with our group. I must tell you that Mark and his company are doing very well with this out-of-the-box idea. Thanks for sharing, Mark.

Guidelines For Using Groupon and LivingSocial Type Services

- Never offer this during your busy season. If you go with this type of offer, make the offer during your slow months.
- I would suggest limiting the number you sell to 100.
- I would have the offer expire in 60, 90, or, at the long side, 120 days, and only if offered at the beginning of your slowest season.

- Try and negotiate with Groupon. I have heard that they will sometimes take a tad less than 50 percent of your offer. It's at least worth trying.
- I am repeating this, if you are mobile, walk away from Groupon-style offers, there's simply not enough profit to allow you to go mobile on these offers. Many before you have tried it and are nearly out of business today.

In closing, Groupon and LivingSocial can bring value, but you better set up your offer with the right service at the right price. Also, collecting the contact information, especially the e-mails of those who purchase your offer, should be your top priority. This will allow you to use your newsletter to offer these same people special promotions in the future and sidestep the expensive Groupon and LivingSocial campaigns. Work it right and Groupon and LivingSocial can work for you.

Your Newsletter Efforts

When it comes to one of the most powerful tools within a progressive detailing business, not many tools can compare to this one. I love newsletters. They offer resourceful ways to not only stay connected, but a properly built newsletter also educates, informs, and provides your client base with a way to learn more about you, your services, auto-related topics of interest, and local events. If you build a fact-filled, fun, and educational newsletter, the payoff can be monumental. They say challenge can bring good change and when the world started facing nasty economic times, the expense of a mailed newsletter became unrealistic. So, I had been playing with electronic newsletter systems like Constant Contact and let me tell you, I quickly fell in love. I have tested, changed, toyed with, and sent every kind of newsletter you can think of—all electronically for under $50 a month. Here are some pointers for your newsletter:

- Make it electronic, forget mailing a newsletter, it's just not effective.
- Make sure your company's branding is included on your newsletter.
- Make a customer of the month, every month, and market that customer of the month via your website, newsletter, and local press releases.
- Include links to local events.
- Share links back to your site.
- Make posts that a wide range of people can appreciate.
- Don't offer too much info, keep to a key point. I like to have no more than three headers within my detailing newsletters, like the following:

1. A fun link about an interesting story or local event.
2. Our special offer this month.
3. Our customer of the month.

■ I like to promote gift cards via my newsletter. Here are the holidays where I promote gift cards:

1. Christmas
2. Valentine's Day
3. Mother's Day
4. Father's Day
5. Customer Birthdays

■ I send out my detailing newsletters every three weeks as this allows more opportunity to sell on the holidays I have listed for you.

Success with your newsletter will not happen overnight, so you need to be dedicated to the long-term efforts that a newsletter will require.

The Power of the Press Release

Some of you may say that a press release is old-fashioned or out of date. I hate to tell you pessimists that you are not just wrong, you are missing a very powerful marketing opportunity. I am no press-release expert, but my friend Kimberly Ballard of Kimberly Writes Creative, a professional writer and the official press release writer of The Air Force One Detailing Team, is. Kimberly shared some insight into press releases so get out your highlighter and take some notes.

Rather than struggling to find cost-effective, alternative means for marketing and building awareness, start submitting professionally written and distributed press releases. Using the power of the press is the most inexpensive and widespread means for promoting your business locally, regionally, statewide, and nationally.

Posting them on your website is a magnet for search engines; leave copies on your countertop or include them in a sales/marketing package. Press releases show you to be a subject matter expert (SME), and when editorial writers need sources for stories, they turn to people who regularly send them information about their business. It gives you credibility, and everyone loves a good story.

Thinking only large businesses have anything newsworthy to share is nonsense. Here is a list of newsworthy announcements that almost any small business experiences:

- *Did you just open your doors? The press is interested in any story that shows a contribution to economic growth in your area.*
- *Are you celebrating your first full year in business? How about five years, ten years, twenty-five years or more? Success stories inspire others. Magazines and newspapers are interested in that. How did you overcome obstacles? How did you get through rough economic times? What have you done to consistently grow and build a reputation?*
- *Are you involved in community events? Have you made any charitable donations?*
- *Have you attended any trade shows or sponsored/participated in any events like car shows, golf tournaments, etc.?*
- *Have you won any awards or recognitions?*
- *Did you just purchase cutting-edge equipment, start carrying a new line of products, introduce new techniques or technology?*
- *Are you having a celebration, giving something away, reviving a popular seasonal or annual event?*

Finally, hire an experienced writer to help you write and distribute the press releases. A press release is not an advertisement and if it sounds like one, it will be discarded. A press release should tease a reporter into a bigger story about your business or your involvement in your industry. It should have one major focus and be submitted in a professional format.

In addition, a professional will send your press release down the proper newsroom and editorial channels. For instance, calling or sending a press release to your favorite news anchor or editorial writer is less likely to get coverage because anchors and writers take assignments from editors and the news desk.

One of the biggest challenges you will face is marketing. You could waste tens of thousands of dollars in marketing that will take you nowhere and fast. How do I know? I am a living example of marketing done wrong and I am buddies with many who have paid the same high price I have. Now we all have the same thing in common: We no longer waste huge amounts of cash on marketing.

Let me add that there is no magic bullet for marketing your detailing business, no one way to make you a millionaire. Those detailing pros who are successful tap into the Internet and social media while also mastering old, faithful marketing methods that have been used for longer than you or I have been around.

A word of caution: I see people coming into detailing as cyber junkies, thinking they can rely on web-based marketing alone. That is a terrible misconception. Likewise, others who start detailing businesses and think they can do so without online efforts typically fail.

Today, you need a great personality, the ability to connect with people, and a solid understanding of online marketing. You also need to go old school by maintaining connections within your community. Let's talk about the areas of marketing most overlooked and how you can tap into them to realize a high level of success.

Reputation

Building a reputation does not happen overnight. But your reputation starts with your very first customer. In detailing, many assume that reputation relates to high-end performance, luxury, and exotic cars. That assumption is on target if you set up in Miami, West Los Angeles, or other areas of the world where these types of vehicles are common.

In the rest of the world, you want to concentrate on vehicles that are common and desirable for that market. If you are in Buffalo, Oklahoma, where there is not a single Lamborghini, why would you try to make your name by having a website, business card, or handout with a picture of a Lambo on it? Buffalo, Oklahoma, is all about American-built pickup trucks and American-made sedans. If you market the before-and-after photos of a nice truck that is clean and shiny, people in Buffalo, Oklahoma, will see value in you. Don't market fancy within an average market and don't market average services within an elite-level market. Relate to your market and odds are, they will relate to you. Be known for quality. Be known for detailing knowledge and be likable. That's how you build your reputation.

Perceived Value

I love the saying that "image is everything" and that if you are going to be a successful detailing business owner, you will need to live, eat, and breathe your image. I don't care how basic you are when starting out. Your image, the way you dress, and your equipment need to look clean and professional. People will pay crappy-looking professionals but your staying power will be minimal. You need a cutting-edge detailing system with a good, clean, and professional image to survive. You need to convey that you are "detailing educated" and that you are an expert within your market. You need to look, sound, act, and be the go-to guy or gal in your market. Being the top of mind detailer in a local market is not an easy process and it takes time and effort to achieve. You also need to be dedicated to this process over the long run. I am not talking weeks or months but years. Your knowledge and professionalism will spread across your market one car guy and gal at a time. And as your perceived value grows, you become more valuable to prospective customers.

Trust

Over my career, I have been able to connect with a wide range of customers; everyone from everyday people like you and me, to super-celebrities and business leaders. The one thing they all have in common is trust. When your client (see my explanation of "Client versus Customer" on page 157) starts to view you as not simply a service provider, but a trusted friend within the community your relationship changes, putting you in a very rewarding position. Trust within a business-based relationship brings many benefits.

Client versus Customer

Trust Brings A New Level of Admiration—When you gain a client's trust, you gain friendship, respect, and a desire to help you in your business. When a client admires you, your work, and your work ethics, that level of trust and admiration is a game changer.

Trust Brings Conveniences—When I started to get garage codes and/or security codes for alarm systems, it made it easier on both my client's schedule and my own schedule, as it allowed for me to get the work done on my time rather than theirs. It also showed that I was gaining trust in a big way and that the client appreciated me as a professional, as a person, and as a member of the community.

Trust Brings Referrals—Simply put, when people trust you, they share your business, your services, and your abilities with others. People who buy detailing services from you will most likely have friends and family who will also buy detailing services from you.

Trust Brings Profits—When you are trusted, it comes with responsibilities to do what's right and always offer value. When you offer value and have a client's trust, they will listen to the service suggestions you make. Add in the better service that trust brings, such as having keys to garages and the ability to be a tad more flexible, and trust means profits. Trust should be a major priority in your client relationships.

Trust Brings Satisfaction—When I am trusted to the core by clients, my satisfaction in my work grows, as does my positive attitude. When you and I as business owners have the right attitude, we tend to get motivated and people pick up on that attitude. It's contagious.

Connection

Author Jeffrey Gitomer has a wonderful quote I love: "Customer satisfaction is worthless. Customer loyalty is priceless." I think connecting with clients is one of the most important elements in marketing a business.

When you connect, you lock in the emotional side of people, and you become far more than a detailer to them. When this occurs, you are at a level that makes a relationship bulletproof. Connection means long-term benefits for both you and your clients, which is something all too many detailing pros fail to establish with their client base. Don't make that mistake in your detailing business. Connect in a big way!

Client and Local Market Education

Educating your clients should be very, very important to you. Let's face facts. There are countless detailers out there and we all are aiming to attract new clients while maintaining our current client base. How does one stand out in a large crowd? Naturally, you need to stand out and attract prospective clients. But once contact is made and that client calls or stops by your shop, you need to connect. Education begins at that moment.

Local Car Events

I love these events, I mean love them. I am a classic-car guy. I love old metal and rare cars. Over the years, I have been lucky to own a few cool cars and have had the privilege of taking part in some of the world's best shows, first as a pro detailer working on some really cool vehicles, then as a speaker. My show-and-event experiences date back to the '80s and after all those years, I figured out a few things when it comes to making profits from these events. Here are some facts that I think could make a serious impact on your perceived value, your reputation, and your overall profits:

- Showcase your work and abilities—I like to take a car that is scratched up and has some really nasty paint challenges and get that car to its full potential! But I don't paint correct the entire car; I tape off a couple areas, such as half the hood, half of the trunk lid, and a couple sections on the sides. This allows those visiting our booth to see firsthand the dynamic difference we can make on a vehicle and is a great way to showcase your abilities.
- Get people interested and engage them—One of the best tools we have for shows is a Spin-and-Win prize wheel. These Spin-and-Win prize wheels are mini versions of the *Wheel of Fortune* wheel seen on television. You attach prices and giveaways to the wheel, and I am telling you, this brings people in! The most important element to this is that they need to sign up for the giveaway and provide their e-mail address. I give away a deluxe-level detail to one lucky winner who will be notified via e-mail. For us, we are direct that this also allows them a free subscription to our monthly "Details Newsletter."

- Females rule and guys drool—Having an attractive, professional female within a car event booth is worth the effort. I am talking about an attractive, classy woman who understands at least the basics of your efforts at the event. I can easily double the interest we gain at events by including an attractive, smart female into the mix at events, and I am guessing so will you!

Taking part in these events costs money, and realize that 95 percent or more of the people attending will not be interested in your detailing services. With that in mind, we like to take a few unique auto appearance-care products with us to draw people into our display. If you align yourself with a small, not widely available but good product line, not only could you possibly cover your cost of the event, you could also make a profit. Then, every detail you sell is pure profit all while being seen and noted for being involved in the local car scene.

Being at these local car-related events is how I was able to get my start working on high-end classics and, brother, has it paid off. I also did the same with the aviation, boat, and RV markets. There is no reason why you can't do the same and become the big kahuna of detailing within your local area.

Your Local Mall

You may be thinking, how can I market detailing services at my local mall? Can you say *cha-ching?* Here is what we did:

- We approached our local mall and discussed having a car on display, much like the auto dealerships do. We wanted a car parked in the middle of the main isle with a small, modest kiosk to display products, our cash register, and a credit-card machine.
- We desired to be in place the week leading up to Thanksgiving and our last day was December 31. We were only interested in the holiday traffic, no more, no less.
- We worked a deal out with a well-known car dealership and were able to obtain a very nice used black car. The dealership plates were left on and we set up a nice display for their literature as a way of thanking them for giving us the car to use.
- We then carefully taped off the entire car in a checker board pattern. What we did then was make a patchwork or checkerboard effect by polishing every

other section to perfection. So, one square would have swirls and scratches while the squares on either side were better than new. I then staged low-heat lighting around the car so the lighting highlighted the differences in each square.

- The effect was simply breathtaking and it drew a great deal of people into the area. On the busy days, I would act out as if I was polishing, but in reality the mall would not let us do so during business hours. But just turning on the equipment would draw in people like bees to honey!

Our mall goals were simple.

1. We wanted to sell holiday gift certificates for detailing services.
2. We developed a special holiday Car Care Kit designed especially for the mall customer. See the details of this kit below.

Our mall effort was not only a success, but we were able to obtain nearly 300 new e-mail addresses and ended up with many new detailing clients. We had our largest year of gift certificates ever and we had a blast doing it. It was a ton of work and a labor of love, but I had one of the best holiday seasons ever thanks to some of the people we met during this event.

Car Care Kit

This kit included:

- A five-gallon bucket to store the kit
- Quart of car shampoo
- Quart of polish
- Liter of paint sealer
- Bottle of interior cleaner
- Bottle of leather conditioner
- A set of paint-perfection microfiber towels

Localized Networking

There is an old saying, "It's not what you know, but who you know." Let's take that one step further, "It's not who you know, but who knows you!" Being connected and having a nonpaid army of salespeople is what proper networking is all about. When you start marketing, part of the plan needs to be connecting with every business in your area. I start with the local auto industry and drop off a flyer to every mechanic, service center, and auto supply store I can find. If they have anything to do with automobiles, they need to see you and you need to repeat this step at least two to three times a year. Even after fourteen years in my home market, I would get out and drop in on every auto-related business in town each quarter. I made it a point to be active within the local car scene and see the car guys on a regular basis.

Tapping into Localized Lead-Generation Groups

You may or may not be familiar with lead-generation groups. For those who are not, I would advise you to get acquainted with this resource as soon as possible. Want to use a well-proven system for working a leads group and have success within the groups you join? Get to know everyone in the group. As humans, we can be shy and have a tendency to latch onto the first person we get to know in a new environment. This is the worst thing you could do. Work the room, get to know everyone in the group and what they do. Here's how:

- Take Notes—I am terrible with names but never forget a face or what someone does for a living. When I join a group my number one priority is to get business for others but to do that, you need to know what others do, then study how you can help them. Too many people joining groups make it all about themselves. So make your mission to arrive and be accepted within the group. Your goal is to help others. Many times I visit members of the group at their places of business or meet one-on-one with members to learn and share with them. Get to know people. Show a sincere interest in their business.
- Get Involved—These groups are like any organization and if you want to gain members' respect, especially if you are young, get involved. Show the elite members you are real and you are dedicated. When you are engaged, people will engage you. Be active!

- Link Up—One of the first things I do with other local businesses is get them on our website and us on theirs. Linking local sites is a tremendous advantage to your online efforts.
- Showcase—When you are dealing with networking partners who are taking an interest in your business, promote them on your website, within your blog, on Facebook, within your newsletters, and most importantly, share them with your customers.
- Establish a Group Commission—Want a commission-based sales force? Offer a commission to those within the group! Within my leads group and the chamber of commerce, I give each member a 10 percent commission and when they reach ten paying referrals, I detail a car for them at no charge. I want their business and I want them making money off me. I also want the referral business that their referrals will bring me.
- Attend Everything—When I am building a business or opening a new location, I am out three to four times a week at events. I work long-and-hard hours getting connected and you will need to do the same. You can skip these events and be average, but if you want to grow your business and grow it at the fastest level possible, it is going to take this level of activity to make it happen. Take on this challenge and realize far-above-average growth. I have tried both roads, people, and I can tell you, the hard work will pay off if you are devoted and smart.

Your Local Chamber of Commerce

Your local Chamber of Commerce can most likely fit into one of two categories: on fire or dead. A chamber that is active with a large membership can help you build your business. If your chamber has little or no involvement in the community and a nonexistent membership, don't waste your time.

With today's economic conditions, many chambers of commerce are rethinking their goals and the impact they can have on local communities. I am hearing, seeing, and experiencing the encouraging trend that chambers of commerce are setting for their memberships and communities. I have a newfound respect for the Chamber of Commerce and am very active within my local chamber. I believe you should also get involved.

When it comes to progressive chambers, I love the fact that many offer newsletters to their members and many offer a free ad for new members. I can do a lot with a free introduction ad and given that their month-to-month ads are affordable, this is another bonus when it comes to a good organization. This is a great opportunity to both network and market your detailing business.

Radio Advertising

Radio advertising is like hitting the craps table in Vegas, you can get lucky and take some money home or you can lose it all. With that said, if you run the right ad, on the right station for your market, and negotiate the right deal, radio can pay off. Here are a few notes and suggestions for radio advertising:

- When I think radio and detailing, I think of Rick Dees, a radio DJ on KIIS FM in Los Angeles. Back in the '80s Rick, one of the most listened-to DJs in one of the largest markets in the world, would go on the air and mention his recent detail performed by Steve's Detailing. Steve's Detailing was being highlighted by one of the biggest names in radio. Who is your local Rick Dees and can you get him/her talking about you?
- We have duplicated this in a couple of markets, including our local market in Southern California where the local TV/radio host interviewed us live on the air. It may take a few detailing services to show off your talents and abilities, but if you do it right with the right radio personality, the payoff could be substantial.
- Almost every radio station has a van and this could offer a great opportunity for trade work. You detail the van on a regular basis and they run your ads.
- Selecting the station you advertise on is hugely important. If you are in a market where country music is popular and the most listened-to station in town is a country music station, guess where your radio efforts should be? Advertise on the stations your prospective clients listen to—the stations that will bring in money.
- The time of day your ads are run is important. The morning and afternoon commute to and from work is the time that is most desirable.
- The voice that makes your ads is an important element of your radio advertising. If your local station does not have a hugely popular radio personality, make the ad spots yourself. Remember, the local DJs are heard all day long so their voices blend into just another ad and yours won't stand out. If you are comfortable record your own ad. If you have a well-

known-and-respected local radio personality and he or she is willing to make a spot in the form of a testimonial about your detailing services, that is powerful.

■ Negotiating is key within any advertising deal. Don't roll over and accept the offer they make, counter that offer. These days, good advertisers are hard to find so do yourself a favor and play hardball on the price.

Newspaper Advertising

Newspapers, especially daily papers, are one of the worst forms of detailing advertising that I have seen. If you are in a small-to mid-size market that has a weekly paper, that is a step above, but in general, newspaper advertising is too costly with too low of a return for us detailers.

Yellow Pages

If you are in a very small market and the ad is cheap, maybe. If you are in a mid-size-to-large market, not only no, but absolutely no.

Local Magazines and Printed Publications

When I opened shop, I had every local publication approach me, all offering huge success and massive amounts of exposure. I tested a few and the outcome versus the cost was dismal at best. Again, I am much more open to keeping with forms of advertising with higher returns and local magazines are not one of them.

Direct-Mail Marketing

Mailing out to local households in your area is something that many new to detailing think of doing in the early stages of their business or as a way to receive a quick-and-fast injection of new customers. This can be a costly mistake. Direct-mail marketing can and does work, but at what cost? To perform direct mail the right way, you need to realize that it takes repetitive mailings to achieve moderate to solid returns. Performing multiple mailings in mass numbers has proven time and again far too costly for most detailing professionals. Let's look at some facts about direct-mail marketing:

■ If you are going to perform a direct-mail marketing campaign, do it right. Don't buy into direct-mail services. Few if any understand our industry and will lead you astray.

- If you are going to purchase a mailing list, do so by contacting a company that can provide you a list based on of the make, model, and year of vehicle most likely to purchase detailing services. For instance, for the last list I purchased, I hired PostcardMania to supply me with 2008 to 2012 BMW 5 and 7 series cars, 2008 to 2010 Mercedes Benz E and S class, and 2008 to 2010 Audi A6, A8, and R8 vehicles within the desired zip codes. PostcardMania was able to build us a list with some four hundred names and addresses to which I marketed. The return versus the investment was fair to average. I would do this again but only if I really needed the new client base as this is still a very costly form of marketing.

I am all about mail marketing, but I prefer to use my organic list built from clients I have already done business with. This list is from our current client base and is a very effective way to keep in contact with your client base.

SendOutCards

One of the coolest marketing tools I have ever seen is SendOutCards. At first, SendOutCards services looked costly and was marketed like a multi-level marketing (MLM) organization, which at first turned me off. Then my buddy Jim started using the system and I performed some research and found that my original ideas were wrong. The SendOutCards services are unreal. It makes follow up and keeping in contact with your client list easy and very professional. You can print custom greeting cards with photos of your clients' cars (or better, your client posed in front of their car) all for less than what a greeting card would cost at your local card store.

I use the SendOutCards service within my daily micromarketing efforts that we will cover later in this chapter. If you don't think sending out greeting cards is valid or important, do yourself a favor and do an Internet search on The World's Greatest Salesman, Joe Girard. Joe made a career that few within the auto sales industry have or will ever see again. In great part, Joe is a firm believer in keeping in contact with

> The elevator to success is out of order. You'll have to use the stairs, one step at a time.
>
> —*Joe Girard*

his clients and did so with thank-you and greeting cards. You can be at the top of your game with massive success by doing what Joe did and SendOutCards makes it much easier and more affordable. The average marketer does not send follow-ups, thank-you cards, or greeting cards. The successful entrepreneur does.

Signage for Your Building or Mobile Unit

Let's start with your mobile unit. Most think "big" when they think mobile detailing systems. I think practical, economical, and image. I am all about these systems telling my story and with modern-day vinyl wraps, you can take an ordinary vehicle and make it a first-class detailing system. Don't think colossal big, think operational and think image. These days I am eco-friendly and using smaller vehicles for mobile detailing. Here are a few examples of vehicles we are using or seeing as mobile detailing platforms and how we treat the signage:

- Various Half-ton Pickup Trucks—I started out using a truck to tow the detailing trailer. Now, the truck is the detailing system. Add on a shell or tonneau cover and a few cool little tricks and you have a fully capable detailing platform to work from. I like the shell option due to the fact that it allows more surface to apply a wrap and therefore offers a larger moving billboard.
- Ford Transit Van—A teacup-size van that can offer you all the conveniences of a van, but smaller. This is a very nice mobile option.
- Chevy HHR Panel Utility—Compact and very eco-based. I have built a couple mobile systems with the HHR Panel and they are cool. You can't take a ton of stuff, but if you are a one- or two-man operation, I love this model.
- Toyota FJ and Honda Element—I am building two systems now, one with a Toyota FJ with a small pull-out unit in back and an eco-box and also the same set up with a Honda Element. Both are super cool and very affordable builds. These systems are based on a low volume, high-quality detailing business. Very unique with lots of cool factors.

A mobile unit, no matter what make, model, or style you go with all have the same opportunity for you. They offer the chance to create a moving billboard for all to see as you drive or park the vehicle around town. Today, you have many options for signage on your mobile detailing unit. My favorite is the full wrap.

Let's talk about your fixed location. If you have a building, especially if your site has solid traffic passing by it, you need to take advantage of that by getting the right

Signage Examples

Full Wrap

The full-wrap option is eye-catching and you can get super creative on the design. The one drawback, a full wrap can get expensive and the lifespan can be as short as four to five years.

Lettering

Another option for your mobile unit signage is to have lettering and limited graphics added. You can still get attention with this design and the investment is much more realistic.

signage out front. Before you jump on putting a sign out front of your new location, you may have a few hoops to jump through before the sign goes up. Let's review:

1. You need to check with your city and county on sign ordinances. Some cities and counties are pretty picky about signage and therefore you need to do a little research.

2. Tell your message. Your name is important but what you do could mean even more. One sign I installed did not even have our logo on it, it just said "Get Your Car Waxed" and it drew people in. Remember, some people have no clue what the term detailing means but everyone knows what it means to wax your car.

3. Also think about branding inside of your shop. Think of the photos you intend to use in your waiting room. How can you brand the inside of your shop?

4. Also, at every shop I have owned, I always have our mobile unit parked out front as well as around town and at key spots where my ideal clients can see it. If my mobile unit is not out making money, I use it as a rolling billboard.

5. You only have so much signage space on your building, so why not put a daily specials sandwich board out front? Also, when I complete a detail, we park that completed car out front with the tires on red carpets and a sandwich board in front of it saying, "Want Your Car To Look This Good?" and it works. We attract a higher level of client with this method and it's a cheap form of advertising as sandwich boards are inexpensive to have made.

6. You can host an event. I love hosting car shows, how-to clinics, and other vehicle related events at my shops. Make sure you advertise this and get a banner out front with the dates of the event!

Marketing your detailing business never stops and every aspect of your business needs to incorporate marketing and attraction factors into it. Marketing is

Detailer Tip

A fixed location can offer you great signage options. While cities may require signage fees, you can use portable signs, attention-getting banners, and even your own mobile detailing van or SUV as a movable sign in front of your shop. Get creative!

so important and that is why I have two chapters covering online and traditional methods of marketing. Every breath of your business (and personal) life should be marketing-and-sales-based. I never remove my marketing and sales caps, I wear them 365 days a year and you need to be that dedicated to your business too!

> **What is Compounding?**
>
> Let me provide you with Webster's definition:
> > To increase, augment, deepen, enlarge, or grow

Client Compounding

Additional customers mean more than you know. If you are operating a productive referral program, those additional customers are going to assist you in compounding your customer list.

Now, if you are offering detailing, you are going to get detailing customers, right? If you kick off the micro-marketing I just described, you are going to start seeing some amazing results over weeks, months, and, ultimately, years. You are going to gain referrals, you are going to get more repeat business, and your profits are going to grow. That is compounding clients.

Like investing in stocks, mutual funds, or just socking money away in your savings account, you can grow your customer base when you have the proper referral system in place and are performing your micro, online, and offline marketing with vengeance. I mean you need to be screaming your messages loud. We are a busy generation and there is a great deal of noise competing for our attention, so you need to make sure your marketing efforts are screaming.

Micro-Marketing: Your Daily Efforts to Fast and Furious Success

I am going to lay out one to two hours of your day right here and now. Micro-marketing is your daily actions with each and every customer and also includes your blogging, social media marketing, and your referral system, all wrapped up in a very short timeframe each and every business day. Here are your daily steps:

- Make sure you answer your business phone and answer it correctly. Later in the sales chapter, we are going to talk about phone skills within detailing.

- Twenty-four hours prior to a scheduled detailing appointment, call to remind your client of his/her appointment. This one step will assist you at not losing work due to missed or forgotten appointments.
- Take before and after photos of each and every detail you perform and maybe even a little video too.
- When the detail you are working on is complete, there are additional actions you will want to take. These are numbered below:

1. Make certain to leave a thank-you card in the car with a handwritten note. Here is a sample of what I write within the thank-you card.
   Mr. and Mrs. Jones,

   We know you have choices when it comes to your detailing services and Diane and I appreciate your trusting us with your vehicle. Your business means the world to us and so does your sharing our name and services with the family and friends you think would enjoy our detailing services.

   Take care, Renny

2. Leave three business cards inside the thank you card, one for the client and two for them to give away. I have been doing this for almost thirty years and it works.
3. Almost everyone's center console is a mess, so I just plop a business card right down into the side of the center console. Weeks, months, or even years later when they are cleaning out the console, all of a sudden they reconnect with us and bingo, it's time for a detail.
4. Open the glove box, take out the owner's manual, and behind the clear plastic, insert a business card. This way, if the vehicle is sold, your card goes along with it and the new owners will know who has been maintaining the vehicle.
5. Before you leave, if the client is there in person, thank them and ask for referrals. How I do this? "Mr. Jones, thank you for your business. It's a joy to work with clients like you and please, we are a small family business and your referrals to family and friends mean the world to us."
6. Leave a candy or gift bag behind with a business card and maybe a gift card promotion. We like hard candies as they won't melt or freeze and everyone loves hard candy.

- That evening when you get in front of a computer, go to the SendOutCards website and send the clients from today all a greeting card. Include before and after pics so the client can see the difference. If at all possible, include the client in the after pic. If you are able to get a picture of your client, make sure the photo gets in their card.
- Each day, try to make a blog post. Your goal is one post a day or at minimal, three a week, but if you make one a day, your efforts will pay off.
- Then take the time to make a post on your Facebook page.

- The next morning call every detail you performed the previous business day.

> *"Mr. Jones, this is Renny. I detailed your car yesterday. I am following up to make sure you are 100 percent satisfied. Are you enjoying your detailed car?"*

This is over-the-top cool as so few people follow up this way anymore and it shocks and delights people. Also, this gives your client permission to complain. Maybe you left a little something out or left the windows smeared. The best thing

Handling a Bogus Complaint

What happens when you get a bogus complaint like the following:

Client: *"Well, Renny, I am disappointed that I still have some scratches in my paint and a few stains on the interior; other than that, I am happy."*

Reply: "Mr. Jones, if you recall, we spoke about going with our stage III exterior and interior but you felt that was over your budget. I did clearly state that going with our stage II would make your vehicle nice and clean, but imperfections would still be noticeable."

Client: *"Renny, I understand. I was just hoping you could spend a little more time on it and get it all perfect."*

Reply: "I understand, Mr. Jones, but that would be like going to a restaurant and ordering a hot dog and expecting a steak for the same price. I can't afford to give away my time for free but I would be happy to come out and perform the stage III on both the exterior and interior for the amount we spoke about; would that work?"

Some people will complain no matter what you do. But most of the time when we place the follow-up call, people are so excited that we followed up, the conversation gets very positive. Clients are happy to see your level of dedication.

would be to fix it. If you handle this complaint with class and fix it fast, it will create one of the best customers you have. People love dedication and knowing even if you make a mistake, you will handle it.

- Every three weeks, send out a newsletter using the Constant Contact system. This is a great way to keep in front of your client base.
- Every ninety days, use SendOutCards and send postcards to everyone. All you need to send is a nice, random message so people know you are thinking of them.
- Every six months, review your ACT Software and if someone has not used you within six months, send another postcard reminding them it's time for a detail.
- Four weeks before each of the following holidays—Christmas, Valentine's Day, Mother's Day, Father's Day, and a client's birthday—start promoting your gift card sales.

Micro-marketing is all about keeping you in contact with your client base. Staying in constant contact with clients will pay off in more ways than you could dream. Dedicate yourself to the daily and regular functions outlined above and the results you could realize will make a noticeable difference in your business.

Start Screaming!
No one should be as loud and outspoken about your business as you. Today, we live in a noisy society and getting attention has never been more challenging.

Your Inner Circle
The best place to start your detail marketing screamfest is within your family and circle of friends. Have a soft grand opening and showcase your mobile equipment to all you know. Have a car half detailed showing off your capabilities. Don't have

---

Tools For Your Micro Marketing Efforts

1. SendOutCards: Go to www.sendoutcards.com to learn more
2. ACT Software or MS Outlook: Search the Internet for these options
3. Constant Contact: Search www.detailingsuccess.com for special offers

a shop? Host it at a local business or at a car club night at a local diner; get creative and get people seeing your mobile system. If you are starting a fixed location, this is a serious opportunity to have an open house with family and friends, and to ask for input before you do the official open house.

Connecting with Your Local Automotive Industry

Ground and pound at this point. When I moved back to Southern California this last year, the first thing I did was meet the local auto industry players. Make friends in the local industry and not only will you make money, your work will be a blast!

It's Not Who You Know, But Who Knows About You

By getting out and becoming known and likable, people will share your name and services with others. Just like when you put money in the bank and it pays you interest, when you are well known, your reputation, business, and profits are compounded. I love compounding new clients as this is the best form of growth a small business could wish for. It develops clients already sewn into the fabric of your business as they came from a personal suggestion from someone they trust. How can you as a business owner beat that level of connection? You can't.

Going Viral Within Detailing

Get your website up and running, get connected on Facebook and on Google Places, and get your YouTube channel going with a couple of simple videos. Going viral is all too easy today for you to ignore it and it is a sales staff that works 24/7, and for pennies a day.

Days, weeks, and maybe months have now turned into a dream, a passion into a new business venture, and it's time to open your doors and start performing details for paying customers. How exciting! I recommend that you start slow and don't overextend yourself with a tight schedule the opening couple of weeks of your business. Give yourself some time to work into your new business and make sure you have the proper detailing systems and processes in place.

Start With Some Practice Details

Before you get neck-deep into the detail thing, practice! Practice on friends' cars, family members' cars, and start timing your efforts. If you are not trained or if you have never performed at the professional level within a detailing business, you are going to need a lot of practice. If you are not formally trained, I would suggest you detail ten to twenty cars before you even think about taking on paying clients.

Setting the Bar at the Right Level

Show-car detailing, concours-level detailing, super exotics, the rarest muscle cars in town, and the finest vehicles in the world are your goal. Reality check: Are you nuts? Work up to that level, don't set yourself up for steep challenges, start with lower-end vehicles with some serious challenges. I am talking about cars that have scratches from head to toe, interior gunk up to the headliner, and smell like a dead sewer rat.

Plus, few markets in the world have the super cars so widely available that you can make a living working on that level of car. If you do live in an area that will support super high-end detailing, pay your dues on the challenges daily drivers offer and build up your skills.

Most pro-level detailers work on daily drivers and therefore make a living off of these types of cars. Wanting to work on the high-end cars is a fun goal, but hone your skills on the everyday vehicles before you move up to the super exotics.

At this point your quality and skill building is top priority, and as those priorities take form, start working on your timing and efficiency. This is where your detailing systems and processes come into play.

Working Your Referral System

To this day, I work my referral system for my business like a mad dog. Each and every person you come in contact with in the early days of your business needs to understand what you do for a living, so be bold, ask for business. Talk about their car and let them know how good it will look when you get done with it. No one else is going to be this bold about your business, but you better be. Some may call this bold, maybe even aggressive? Develop a classy way of talking, visiting, and getting into a conversation about cars. I am a car guy to the bone. I live, eat, and love everything about the automobile. Funny thing is, when you find a fellow car guy, having a fun conversation that works into your business is not all that hard to master. So start practicing and go get referrals.

Track Every Client You Do Work For

Don't make the mistake I made. For the first couple years in business, I kept basic records, but not at the level I should have. There is a form that I use to collect client

What I Wish I Had Known Before I Started My Business

Matthew Gillican

I would have taken the time to learn how to sell and run a business. Learning the technical part is very important, but learning how to sell and run the business should be a priority along with building the business. I would not settle for a few accounts, I would always be looking for more customers, and not settle for a few customers to keep busy. It's great to have regular accounts, but if something happens and they decide to change (e.g. bring in someone cheaper or use someone else, etc.), it can really affect your financial status when you don't have a steady stream of business coming in from other areas.

data. This is best done with software such as ACT or MS Outlook. See appendix B for a sample client check-in form.

Image Is Everything

You want to look good—really good—from the very first day you start detailing. Here are a few tips:

- Your mobile system or shop needs to be cutting-edge and professional. This does not mean you need to spend a ton of money, but you need to get creative. I was on a serious budget when I got going so I built my mobile system myself to save money. I purchased a reasonable truck to build that platform on. My first mobile system cost me under $6,000 total and it was really cool. I had comments on my mobile system almost daily and that system won me many, many new clients.
- Your cards, flyers, and support material all need to be professional. Don't go online and build cheap-looking items. Spend a little money and get these items done right. You can still have your support items done for cheap, just don't let them look cheap.
- Invest in uniforms. I am a firm believer in having branded shirts. Go with both a collared shirt and T-shirts. I like the look of a collared shirt, but T-shirts can be an effective marketing tool. Look around the industry and you can find some creative ideas of how to make a T-shirt work. For you one-man shops, you can have as little as one shirt made if you are on a budget and there are some great one-off T-shirt sites on the web. For up to five shirts, here are two online options: www.cintas.com for collared shirts and www.impressink.com for T-shirts and sweatshirts.

Branding

Your name, logo, and support materials must look fantastic, and they need to stand out. Take time naming your business and be very particular about your logo and

> Make a little, sell a little, take small steps.
>
> —*3M Corporation Creed*

branding. Don't copy other detailers, be creative. To help with your creative efforts, turn to mycroburst.com. This site lets designers bid on your logo and creative needs. It is very affordable and very effective. Go check it out!

Fire the Boss, But Don't Rush It

Don't fire your boss right away, keep at least a part-time job until your business takes off. If you have some back-up capital that will sustain you, set a limit on how much of that capital you are going to spend before you go get a part-time job. Don't go into debt and don't waste your savings. Your first couple of years are going to be lean and if you plan for it now, you will be a much happier camper when you still have some money in the bank!

12 Establishing a Solid Sales System

Can you sell? Have you ever sold anything before? If you said no, you are confused. As soon as we start preschool we start our career as salespeople. Even at four years old, we all sell ourselves to those around us. As we age, we sell on a more constant basis, so while you think you are not a salesman, in reality you have been selling yourself, your thoughts, your dreams, and your abilities your entire life.

Now, you will need to bring your life experiences together and function as a full-time salesman. Owning your own business means needing to be comfortable selling not only your services, but selling your abilities and yourself as a professional.

People coming to you are looking for a detail but in reality, most are buying you, the service provider. Zig Ziglar has a great quote about salesmen: "Timid salesmen have skinny kids." There is no skinny in detailing, you either make it or you don't. Don't be timid and don't underestimate how important your ability to sell will be within your detailing business.

Detailer Tip

Welcome to sales. Get comfortable with it, get good at it, and get selling now. If you don't get comfortable and talented within your sales efforts, your competition surely will.

Hone In On Your Phone Skills

No matter if you are a mobile operator or a fixed location, your phone skills are very, very important to your overall success. Here are a few pointers on being more effective on the phone:

- Be prepared and proactive. You are the professional. Take control of the call and lead it through your detailing processes. You are the pro and you need to sound and act the part.

- Introduce yourself as the owner and reassure the caller that you are here to serve their detailing needs. Today, the mom-and-pop, Main Street business is a badge of honor. People like knowing that they are dealing directly with the owner. This gives you a serious edge over the shops who are staffed and run by big companies. You have the connection edge, use it.

- Speak with integrity. People want and desire quality, and you need to sound the part of the very professional, warm, friendly, and knowledgeable detailing pro. Listen for statements that are clear on what is important to them. Be very transparent and direct with your price and be confident when you give your price.

- Be confident, but not cocky. Be cool and able to answer all the hard questions, and be very collected and well versed in your profession. Care about them, compliment their vehicle selection, and show them you are listening. If they keep talking about removing swirls, assure them that you specialize in swirl removal and you will do the work yourself to make certain their vehicle is cared for with the utmost attention.

- Your goal is that when the caller hangs up, your conversation exceeded what they expected and they are impressed. Don't be average and always give your best. Allow them to know that you obviously love what you do.

- Here are a few never-evers:

    1. Never lie.
    2. Never be too busy or distracted to be nice.
    3. Never use a poor-quality phone or a speakerphone.
    4. Never be on the move or driving for sales calls. Pull over and give that call your full attention.

Master Your Diagnostic Sales Techniques

You are in love with detailing, now share that love with a constructive sales system and you will be a giant killer within this industry.

The way to think about diagnostic sales is much like a medical exam a doctor performs. A doctor asks you questions about why you are visiting him/her, if you are experiencing any issues or health troubles, examines you, and takes your vitals. Now liken that process to detailing and you have a great way to correspond with prospective clients. Here is a sample sales script we have used for many years:

Phone Script

You: *Thank you for calling Renny Doyle Detailing, what are we going to shine for you today?*

Client: Hi. I wanted to see if I could get some information on getting my vehicle detailed?

You: *Sure, what kind of vehicle do you drive?*

Client: A Chevy Suburban.

You: *What color is the exterior of your Suburban?*

Client: It's black.

You: *Oh you are going to love me. I specialize in black paint. Are there any issues you need addressed on the outside? And is there any pet hair or kid grime on the inside?*

Client: Well, I have kids but it's not too bad and my dog did jump on the paint and put a few nail scratches in it.

You: *I have four kids myself, so I understand the kid thing, and we can address those nail scratches, so no spills or food in the carpets or on the seats?*

Client: Well I do let them eat in the car, but it's not too bad; just some crumbs, and our black lab does travel with us for our weekend boating trips.

You: *How often do you detail your vehicle?*

Client: Once every year or so.

You: *Based on what you have shared with me and the fact you have both some interior and exterior issues to deal with, I am going to suggest our Stage III detail, let me explain these services to you. We are going to perform a three-step process on the paint, we first wash the vehicle including the wheel wells and under the vehicle. We clean and decontaminate the paint surfaces, then perform a two-stage polishing process on the paint. Following the polish, we apply a paint sealer. We prefer to not use waxes like the other guys because most waxes simply do not last more than about thirty to sixty days. Our sealer lasts anywhere from four to six months, depending on how you maintain your car. We then clean all the bumpers and wheels and dress the tires. Also, any black trim on your vehicle is treated with an exterior trim treatment that cleans and protects the plastic. Do you have cloth or leather?*

Client: Leather.

You: *Great, on the interior, we Q-tip clean all the nooks and crannies and exfoliate and condition the leather with a very nice leather protectant. We utilize a European steam system to clean the carpets. This unique system does not leave the carpets soaking wet or smelly like wet extraction does. Wet extracting can cause the carpets to actually get dirtier faster, while our steam system is chemical free and, in many cases, we can remove most stains without the use of harsh chemicals, which is healthier for you and your family. We leave the interior nice and fresh smelling like it was when it was new. The investment for this level of service is $300, based on the conditions you supplied me with today and looking at my schedule, I have an opening on Monday, would you like to get on our schedule?*

Client: Well, I am just checking prices. Thanks for your help.

You: *You are very welcome and we are here to answer any additional questions you may have. By the way, where did you hear about us?*

To Do It All Over Again

Jose Fernandez
Superior Shine Mobile Auto Detailing
Arcadia, CA

My name is Jose "Joe" Fernandez. My company is Superior Shine Auto Detailing based in Arcadia, California. I started Superior Shine full-time in the summer of 1992. Prior to that, I learned my craft growing up at my father's body shop and working at various classic car restorations and customizing shops. Initially, Superior Shine provided auto-detailing services to small body shops and used-car dealers. I have since moved on to detail some of the world's most impressive vehicles and aircraft. My clients include celebrities and multimillionaires with fabulous car collections. I have been fortunate to have worked on historically significant vehicles and aircraft which included many museum pieces. I routinely detail super cars and high-end luxury cars.

If I had it to do over again, I would have learned to be a businessman first. I have spent countless hours washing vehicles to get them spotless without introducing any defects into the finish. I have refined my skills at perfecting paint. I can identify and correct just about any issue in a vehicle's interior, be it stain or mal-odor. I've tested what seems like thousands of paint compounds, and polishing and protection products to find the best. All of these things are important, but I have spent too much time on them. It has been 90 percent of my focus. Detailing skills should actually only maybe get 40 percent of your attention.

I understand now that business requires okay detailing skills, but having sharp business talent is much more important to success than being a super-talented master detailer with lackluster business sense.

I would have gone to school and taken business classes. I would have comprised a business plan. I would have understood profit and loss, forecasting, and my break-even numbers. I would have learned how to select my target market and how to effectively communicate with them.

Making a vehicle perfect is fine, but I would choose making a large profit any day. Can you have both? Yes you can! Also, I would have hired employees much sooner. An employee is an investment. It essentially is unearned income. They sweat, you get paid!

Practice your skills to solve your customers' detailing problems, but don't forget that you're a business FIRST and you must sharpen your business skills as much or if not more than your detailing skills. Get your skills sharp, hire employees, and go out there and grow a successful business!

Using a Little Psychology to Help Sales

Let's tear down the sales script into smaller sections to understand why we ask the questions we ask, and why we are making some of the statements we make:

- Start by answering the phone in a not-so-average way. "Hello" is predictable; everyone answers the phone that way, and you are not everyone. I want you to stand out, and so should you.
- Determine the color of the car. If you find out that the vehicle is black, then state that you specialize in black paint (if that is indeed one of your specialties). This will set you apart from the other guys.
- Go into basics and explain your processes a little to further set you aside from others the caller might speak with.
- Try to speak about longer-last sealers versus inferior waxes, again setting you apart from the other guys.
- Talk about Q-tip cleaning all the nooks and crannies, which is a key term detailing clients like to hear.
- Explain that you utilize a European steam system versus traditional wet extraction. Again, this will distinguish you from the competition, and clean, dry carpets are very attractive to detailing clients.
- At several points, ask about special needs, both for the exterior and interior alike. If the caller leaves something out, this gives you the opportunity to adjust the price based on those needs.
- At the end, alert the caller that you can fit them into your schedule on the first available day. This is a closing and you are asking for the sell and asking the caller to make an appointment.
- If the caller does not accept your scheduling request, thank them for the call and ask them to call you if they have any questions. If you have an opening, ask them one last question, a very important question: "How did you hear about us?" This question is a good one to ask as it is a way to track your marketing efforts and to know if certain clients are sharing your services with others. This one question provides a great amount of feedback on where you should be putting your marketing dollars, but surprisingly, this question can give you something more than marketing data. Almost half of the callers who, moments earlier, were ready to hang up on you will now be ready to schedule. I believe that when you ask them how they heard about you, they

no longer think of you as a salesman, or they realize that whoever referred them trusted you. That creates a connection and they schedule the detail work right then and there.

Work That Menu

As you take calls and meet with people in person, keep your menu in mind. Sell your prospective clients what they need, not what you want to sell them. There will be times to upsell and there are times you should downsell. If you push services that the client is clearly not interested in then you stand to lose the client to future sales.

Printed Menus and High-Tech Options

The days of a printed menu are gone. With iPads and websites the need for a host of printed goods has diminished greatly. Having a nice bifold or trifold menu is a nice addition, but if your budget only allows for print or technology, go with technology. If your budget allows for both, I would suggest both an iPad-based menu and a printed version, but don't include prices. On the printed version, leave an area where you can write in your estimate for the prospective client. Putting prices in print anywhere is a mistake that has been proven time and time again in the nearly two hundred shops I have assisted.

Scheduling Detailing Jobs

After all this talk about technology, your detailing schedule is one area where you should go old school. For years, we have used the same kind of scheduling book hairdressers use. This is a great system that allows you to see your schedule all in one place, and at one time. You can also make adjustments and changes on the fly, and it does not rely on connectivity with your cell phone. We have tried electronic scheduling and for us, the old pencil and paper is more effective.

Hiring Employees

You have opened your doors, your marketing efforts are working, and now it's time to get some help to handle the workload. I take hiring very seriously and I hope you do also. Finding the right person is hard for those of us who own a small business. We have high expectations with staff members. Brace yourself as I must be direct with you: You will never duplicate yourself, so don't expect your staff to be you.

Lighten up and realize that if your staff was just as dedicated to the business as you, would they still be on staff or would they be running their own business? Let's talk about factors, other than pay, that motivate the staff you hire. It's not all about money, you know.

1. Quality of work environment is important. Give your staff a clean, safe, and happy workplace.
2. Quality of life is essential so don't expect your staff to keep the same hours as you or work like you do. I made this mistake and lost some good people. Don't make the same mistake.
3. Be legitimate, take taxes out, and have workers' compensation in place.
4. Health care for families and singles is a huge plus.
5. Time off for vacation is a must. Yes, they need a break!
6. Free family details can be a nice perk. In the off season and once during the summer, we bring in close family members' cars and get them all cleaned up!
7. This one is going to sound strange to you old guys, but here we go: Allow staff to bring an iPod to work. I give them a set of earphones with one earphone cut off. Listening to music is motivation to many and having one earphone missing still allows them to hear what's going on around them. (Check with your local labor board to make sure this does not violate local workers' safety guidelines.)
8. Give them a chance to promote and earn more. Don't be greedy, share the wealth as you become more successful. Give regular raises and make working for you a good thing!

A Great Sales Training Resource

So let's say you need a little practice talking to people. One of the best things I did when I was young was to join Toastmasters (www.toastmasters.org). This is a public speaking group that helped me greatly when it came to speaking to one person or two hundred. Look into this asset. Your first meeting is usually free and Toastmasters is a great resource for helping you become a far better detailing sales professional.

> For every sale you miss because you're too enthusiastic, you will miss a hundred because you're not enthusiastic enough.
>
> —*Zig Ziglar*

When it comes down to it, be yourself. Share your passion, love, knowledge of detailing, and you'll be successful within your sales efforts. It may take practice and some time, but when you really enjoy what you do, keep a positive outlook, and stay positively engaged to your business over the long haul, you will make money and have fun! Detailing is a lifestyle; live it to the fullest.

Myths versus Truths

When you get a couple years into the detailing industry, you are going to realize that half of what you read (aside from what's in this book, of course) is a bunch of bull or so misguided that one could never make a go at detailing with the way most of the profit mongers or e-thugs explain it.

Addiction to Perfection and How It Can Make or Break You

Odds are, if you are getting into detailing, you are a perfectionist. That is a very good trait for detailing, as long as you can control your inner perfectionist. Here are three pointers:

1. Making a Profit—Remember, you are detailing for profits now. Getting a vehicle perfect is fine, if you are getting paid for perfection.

2. Track Your Man-Hours—I have a rule of thumb, if you are a pro-level detailer, you should be producing at a minimum of $40 per man-hour. If you are performing a service solo and you are charging $120 for that service, it should take you no more than three hours to perform it. If you are mobile, you need to include your travel time to and from the site to figure out your true profits. I know for some, this is a strange number, but I have made calculations for years, and the $40 per man-hour has been proven time and again to be a solid baseline for minimal per-hour income to justify your profitability. In your early days, you will be slow and take more time to perform your work but as you grow, learn, and get faster, that $40 per man-hour is a solid goal to aim for. I have included a sample man-hour tracking form for you to copy and use. See appendix B.

3. Don't give your work away—Each market has its glass ceiling on price and every market can be developed and grown to accept more, but it takes time and investment in educating your market over the weeks, months, and years. When I started our office in Sun Valley, Idaho, a signature-level service on both the interior and exterior was $125. Some four years later, that same detail was nearly $400. You can develop a market, it just takes time.

Detailing Is Really All About Paint Perfection

Paint correction is an art when performed at the highest levels. It can take you years to perfect, master, and understand it. We detailers are obsessed with paint correction and paint perfection. In certain markets, the highest level of paint correction and perfection is desired and paid for. For the rest of the world, which is the majority of the detailing community, paint correction is just one element within detailing.

1. While we have determined that paint correction is an art, for the most part, paint systems remain the same year after year. Every five years or so, we have something new come along and yes, some manufacturers have softer paint systems while others have harder paint systems. For those who perform detailing on daily drivers, soccer-mom crossovers, and the everyday cars you and I see daily, performing a concours-level detail is not practical. Who in their right mind would spend $800 to $2,000 on a detail for a daily driver? The answer: no one.
2. The daily driver crowd is not looking for paint perfection, most would not know a perfectly corrected paint system if it was right in front of them. The daily driver crowd and even most of the luxury-car crowd simply want a clean and shiny car.
3. Over my career, at my retail detailing shops, 55 to 60 percent of my clients have been women. Woman clients are very particular about the interior of their vehicles. The vehicle they bring in may be nasty on the inside when they bring it to you, but they expect that interior to be next to perfect when they pick it up.
4. Each new model year, interior surfaces change. This means that every year, we need to make moderate adjustments to our interior detailing methods. Keeping abreast of these new materials, the actions we need to take to clean them, and the reactions the surfaces will have to our efforts are also very important.

My point to all this is, that to be a true detailing pro, you need to be well rounded. You need to see the importance within the art of paint systems correction and perfection while realizing there are many additional elements within your efforts that need your attention.

Build It and They Will Come

Be real with your expectations. You can't just open up a shop, put a sign out, and have people flock to your new detailing business. You need to deliver a very talent-based detail that will take you some time to master. You will need to have many of the systems in place we have spoken about, and you will need to make certain you are using the right equipment and products. In today's detailing game, if you are not performing at the very top, your chances of survival are pretty slim.

My Car Looks Good. I Can Detail Anything, Really.

Detailing your own car, your parents' car, even close friends' cars are all a good start. But once you start getting paid for your services and competing with knowledgeable detailers with years of experience under their belts, it's no longer friendly, helpful, and innocent. It's complex detailing for profit and the game is very competitive, very serious, and very challenging. Be real with yourself and be dedicated to your detailing education; it's going to take every brain cell in your head to make this a true success.

When to Fire Your Boss

The answer is simple: When your detailing has proven that it's a year-round cash flow that will support your income needs. As I discussed earlier I kept a part-time job in the slow, winter months for the first two years. In reality, I should have kept a ten-to-twenty-hour winter job the third winter, but we squeaked by. From the fourth year forward, I kept busy pretty much of the year. Give yourself four to seven years before you are making a rewarding income. Some may be faster, but as a rule of thumb, this is a reality.

Make a Million In Detailing?

Some reading this right now are thinking that they will start a detailing business and be well on the way to becoming a millionaire. If you want to make $30, $40, $60 or $100K a year, that is realistic. But if you are looking to clear hundreds of thousands of dollars in detailing, you need to start up a very large car-wash chain with detail

To Do It All Over Again

Dan Ekenberg

Auto Detailing Network

I am a single father and operated Enchantment Mobile Detailing in Boise, Idaho, from 1993 to 1995. I launched the website Mobileworks in April 1996. The site was largely for the mobile detailing segment of the industry.

The website was renamed Auto Detailing Network in 2010 to accommodate the changing landscape of the industry. The site includes industry news, blogs, and articles from industry leaders. In November 2011, the website autodetailingnetwork.com was launched with an emphasis on detailing products, equipment, business opportunities, and training. I moderate the detailing network group on www.linkedin.com with nearly 1,000 registered members. And I've spoken at detailing events and trade shows on Internet marketing for detailing businesses as well as striking a healthy balance between business and personal life.

When I first began my mobile detailing business in the mid '90s there were not the vast online resources for training, products, etc. as there are today. As a result, I was largely self-taught. Fortunately, I had experience from detailing my own vehicles and my business background was invaluable as I worked to promote my business.

Still, situations would arise where I was not prepared for the challenges I was presented. I recall a specific job regarding detailing a large motor home. When I was contacted about the job I accepted it even though I had no experience detailing such a vehicle. My lack of knowledge caused great frustration for me and my customer and could have cost me and my business dearly.

Had I been better prepared with proper training on procedures and products for such a vehicle, I could have saved a lot of time, money, and frustration. I quickly learned that detailing my own vehicle did not prepare me for the challenges of operating a detailing business. Were I considering starting a detailing business today, I would attend a professional detailing training class before investing any additional time or money.

> I never perfected an invention that I did not think about in terms of the service it might give others. . . . I find out what the world needs, then I proceed to invent.
>
> —*Thomas Edison*

centers attached or find yourself a more profitable business. Detailing is a lifestyle business and while you can carve out a nice life and make a nice living, I have known only a couple people who have made really big money in detailing. Their road was hard and long, and the opportunities within this industry for that level of income is very, very limited.

Using Detailing as a Springboard for New Opportunities

Detailing makes a wonderful first business. Detailing makes a fantastic lifestyle business and, for the most part, detailing is an affordable business to start. It is also a great way to grow into new, bigger, and more profitable businesses. I have taken the earnings from detailing and started other ventures. I know many who have done the same, so keep your eyes open and always be on the lookout for new opportunities. My wife calls me an habitual entrepreneur as I love the challenge of building a concept, getting it to market, and either making the profits from the concept or selling the concept. Does that sound like fun or what?

The Most Important Words of Detailing Wisdom I Can Share With You

Bear with me for just a tad longer. I have a story that I want to share with you and two facts that have kept me in the detailing industry all these years. I have done many things in my life and have lived out many dreams. I have owned several small businesses in my forty-five years on this planet and I have been a mid-level executive for a Fortune 500-level organization. I have been a reserve sheriff's deputy, and a member of two cutting-edge mountain rescue teams. I have been the commander and leader of one mountain rescue team and have risked my life to save others.

Of all the things I have done, nothing, I repeat nothing, has brought me the joy, delight, happiness, and satisfaction that the detailing industry has supplied me.

What I Wish I Had Known Before I Started My Business

Diane Doyle

Many people have no idea about the time and dedication involved in starting, running, and succeeding in business. Being successful in business is a wonderful goal, but make sure you are well-rounded and make part of that goal being a success at home too. So many people make the mistake of working so hard to get the family ahead that they forget to make time (quality time) for family.

Don't work so hard and so single-mindedly that when you reach your goal, you have no one left to share it with. There are so many sayings about spending so much time making money that you never have time to enjoy it. MAKE TIME. Don't look back and have regrets. You set your own hours and make your own schedule, so make time for family too. Don't look back and regret missing special moments with your spouse, children, and grandchildren.

Starting your own business is hard and you must work hard, but don't get tunnel vision. Success has many facets and you must shine all sides. Don't neglect your family.

Don't spend, spend, spend. There are some amazing tools, great products, and cool gadgets out there, several of which will make your business greater, more profitable, and easier and/or more successful. Make a list in several columns and prioritize your spending.

Don't start your business being so far in the red that it will take eons to dig yourself out. You want to own your own business and time, but don't let them own you.

Ease in. You have bills and needs. Make sure that you can satisfy those needs. If you aren't making the big bucks immediately you might need to supplement your income with a part-time job, or don't quit your current position until you have built up clientele. Rome wasn't made in a day. Be patient. Your hard work will pay off if you work smart.

Detailing is a lifestyle. For me (and those I have watched climb the ladder) detailing, the car world, and what we do for a living are part of who we are.

Detailing needs to be a family affair.

Detailing allows me to take part in and enjoy my hobby.

Detailing allows me to live, plan, and enjoy the life I want.

Detailing allowed me to tell my boss to take a flying leap.

Detailing is far more than simply work for me, it is who I am now.

Detailing is a business.

Detailing is wide open for those who have abilities and personalities that win people over.

The reason I have had success within detailing is based 100 percent on two distinct reasons: my passion for the art of detailing, and my need to succeed. I hated corporate America and I am not the guy to have a boss. I wanted more from my life and I wanted to wake every morning wanting to go to work, not dreading that I had to go. Detailing is my work, my way of life, my hobby, and my passion. I am a lucky man to be doing what I love and getting paid to do it.

I have four great kids and when our kids were very young, I realized I wanted to see every step they took. I wanted to be at every teacher conference and every sporting event I could. While my work has, at times, taken me away from my family, the massive amount of time I have had to share their lives and see them grow has been an absolute blessing.

A job was just that, a job. And while I had successes while working for others, I found that I was not the ideal employee as I get restless. I am sure that if you are reading this book, you may suffer from that same restlessness syndrome. First, don't burn bridges and don't be in a race to go into business. Take your time, make a plan, and work your plan. Don't go and piss off your employer. Those same people could have your back if you need help later in life, and could become clients.

I have talked about what makes a good detailer and why you should make sure your WHY is for all the right reasons. Plan on working your tail off and, note to self,

> The detailing industry is in a constantly forward motion. Stand still for a second and you will be left behind.
>
> —*Renny Doyle*

detailing is not glorious unless you make it glorious. Make your detailing efforts just another thing to do and it will be that, just another thing to do. Make detailing a spiritual adventure and you could be writing this book. If you're not spiritual or absolutely crazy about detailing, it could eat you alive.

I leave you with this: Develop your detailing business as an extension of your passion and desire to make more of your life. If you make it all about money, it can upset the overall reasons of why you entered this trade in the first place. Keep detailing purely for yourself. Use detailing as a way to live life, I mean really live, and experience life. Detailing can help you do that if you let it.

Appendix A:
Don't Put It Off, Get Going Now!

Your head may be spinning now, so I was thinking that having some direction and action steps would give you a little more direction in the early stages of your establishing or expanding your detailing business. Here are some basic steps to start working on now, TODAY:

1. Write out a plan, even if it's brief.

2. Make a financial plan.

3. Evaluate your market and the detailers within the market.

4. Think about your detailing education and how you are going to be a top performer. I love the site www.detailingsuccess.com (maybe due to the fact that it's mine).

5. Secure your company name. Think creatively and think long-term goals. Naming the business after you will limit your ability to sell the business, so think local!

6. Think branding. I love the site www.mycroburst.com as a place to get creative logos designed.

7. Name your brand. An example of this was our slogan in our Sun Valley location, "Sun Valley's First Choice In Auto & Corporate Jet Detailing Services."

8. Get your domain locked in. I am very picky about domains and I name my location within the domain. An example of this would be sunvalleyautodetailing.com or bostondetailing.com. The search engines love these domains and you will show up within searches faster and higher if you build your site right. I buy my domains at www.godaddy.com.

9. Start setting up your social media sites such as a business page on Facebook and your channel on YouTube.

10. Get all of your support and marketing materials together and designed. Again, first impressions are everything so make your cards incredible.

11. Are you going mobile or with a fixed location? Start building your system and/or looking at locations for your shop. I remind you, think about your budget and keep in mind that you are going to need some money in the bank to support your business in the opening months. It's going to take time to start making profits and you need to think ahead.

12. Get your products ordered. This is going to be a big step and make sure to check out www.detailingsuccess.com. You can join the Detail Mafia group as an associate member and gain access to the leading products that our team of worldwide pros are using, plus have access to our weekly Tuesday night online webinars. We have industry leaders as guest speakers and these events rock.

13. Practice details and start perfecting your art.

14. Practice your sales approach and vehicle evaluation, both in person and on the phone.

15. Repeat #13 time and time again, over and over as this is vitally important!

16. Get connected within the industry via detailing gurus, forums, and blogs.

17. Get connected locally and start people talking. Start with family and friends, then start joining groups such as the chamber of commerce and leads groups.

18. Start speaking and presenting with car clubs within your local market. Educating your local market and becoming the local detailing guru is massively important.

19. Think about meeting with a CPA and setting up your organization, including your Quickbooks ledger. This is a great investment and something that should be done in the early stages.

20. Have fun and hold on. You are in for a wild ride!

> Just Do It.
>
> —*Nike*

Here are several examples of forms that should become commonplace within your detailing business.

Menu Design
Auto Detailing Services

Express Detail $20-$30	Deluxe Package $60	Exterior Package	Interior Package $135
Hand Wash	Hand Wash	Hand Wash	Meticulous Vacuum
Microfiber Dry	Microfiber Dry	Microfiber Dry	Q-Tip Clean Nooks
Tire Shine	Tire Shine	Tire Shine	Clean Dash
Add Wax	Clean Wheel Wells	Treat Wheel Wells	Clean Door Panels
Starter Package $40	Treat Wheel Wells	Dress Wheel Wells	Dress Interior
Hand Wash	Clean Door Panels	Clay Vehicle	Clean Leather
Microfiber Dry	Clean Dash	Machine Polish	Condition Leather
Tire Shine	Vacuum Interior	Apply Sealant	Multi-step Clean
Interior Vacuum	Clean Windows	Protect Rubber/Plastic	Shampoo Carpets
Clean Dash	Clean Mirrors	Polish Chrome	Steam Clean Carpets
Clean Door Panels	Dress Interior	Rain Repellent	Clean Doorjambs
Dress Interior	Apply Wax		
Clean Windows	Rain Repellent		**Complete Package**
Clean Mirrors			Exterior Package
			Interior Package

The prices shown above are starting costs and may be higher depending on the vehicle's condition.

XYZ Detailing Services

Client Check-In Form

Client Name:_____

Mailing Address:_____

Home Phone:_____

Cell Phone:_____

Work Phone:_____

Description Of Vehicle:_____

• Level of Service Recommended Interior:_____

• Level of Service Accepted Interior:_____

• Level of Service Recommended Exterior:_____

• Level of Service Accepted Exterior:_____

Client E-mail:_____

(You will receive a complimentary edition of "Making the Most of Your New Detail," our downloadable e-book filled with helpful tips, advice, and money-saving offers on all our detailing plans and services. A $20 value—FREE!)

Interior Dressing Preferences:

Exterior Dressing Preferences:

Client Initials:_____

Client Special Request & Notes:

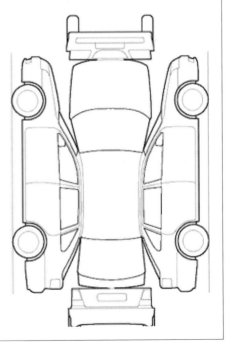

0 = Dent or Ding

⌣ = Scratch

B = Broken

ABC Detailing Services, LLC.

Invoice For Services

Invoice#0131-11

To: Bad Bear Sports Wear
P. O. Box 2225, Big Bear City, CA 92314

Attention: Rick

Boat Detail Included items outlined below

- Pre-treat exterior for deposit removal
- Wet wash
- Clay
- Heavy oxidation removal
- Apply paint protection sealer to exterior
- Install clear coat additive over blue (faded) to slow chalking effect
- Deep clean interior
- Apply marine-grade vinyl protection
- Clean carpets
- Hand wax trailer
- Clean and dress tires and wheels (remove heavy grease from port side rear wheel)

Total $700.00 Minus $100 credit for acid washing lower section

Grand total: $600.00

Submit Payments To:
P.O. Box 1111
Your City
Your State, 92315

abcdetailing.com   ABC Detailing, LLC   (555) 555-1212

VEHICLE EVALUATION

Date _____

Name _____ Phone _____

Address _____ City _____ State _____ Zip _____

E-mail _____

Year _____ Make _____ Model _____ Color _____ Vin# _____

EXTERIOR PAINT	RATE 1-10 (1 BEING FLAWLESS)
Fallout	
Overspray	
Hard Water Spots	
Swirls/Holograms	
Isolated Scratch(es)	
Oxidation	
Stains (i.e. Bird Dropping)	
Acid Rain	
Paint Failure	
Other	
NOTES:	

INTERIOR	RATE 1-10 (1 BEING FLAWLESS)
Soiled	
Isolated Stain	
Scuffs	
Tears	
Faded	
Excessive Odors	
NOTES:	

MISC.	RATE 1-10 (1 BEING FLAWLESS)
Wheels	
Tires	
Moldings	
Glass (Tint)	
Clear Plastic	
NOTES:	

RECOMMENDED SERVICE(S)	PRICE
Ultimate	
Express	
Odor Removal	
Fallout/Overspray Removal	
Clear Plastic Restoration	
Isolated Scratch Removal	
Other	
TOTAL	

Inspected By: _____

Customer Signature: _____

VVEF

Daily and Hourly Profits Worksheet
Sample 1

Day: Monday

Start Time: 8 a.m.

End Time: 5 p.m.

Total Hours = 9 hours (lunch on the run)

Job One: X-Press = $69.00
Job Two: X-Press (same location as #1) = $69.00
Job Three: F150 Deluxe Detail w/ Road Paint Removal = $187.00
Job Four:
Job Five:

Sales Total: $325.00

Divide Total Sales by Total Hours =
($325.00 Divided by 9 hours = $36.11 an hour)

Hourly Income Today = $36.11/hour gross

Older Vehicle Disclaimer and Agreement Form

Date:

Name:

Vehicle Type & Year

VIN:

While Attention To Details and its staff make every effort to protect your car, when we are dealing with cars five years old or older, items can simply break or fail due to the age and/ or condition of the vehicle.

Items such as but not limited to:

Mechanical failure to run or start As vehicles age, things happen. At times vehicles will not start or run and nothing we do during our services can cause this failure. It is simply a mechanical issue. Also, older cars tend to run down batteries quickly and therefore we are not responsible for dead batteries.

Discoloration of surfaces As vehicles age, the colors used on and within the vehicle will become more and more brittle and colors may fade or be removed during detailing, and we cannot take on that liability.

Paint and pinstripes Some older paint and pinstripes can be lightened or removed during the normal detailing process. You are having us perform this work at your own risk.

Delamination/discoloration of plastics, vinyl, leather, metals, and other surfaces Older materials (both interior and exterior) de-laminate and we cannot be responsible for the color, coatings, or finishes on older cars.

Headliner and upholstery sag At times, old material will sag after cleaning and this is simply due to age. Our attempts to revive those materials can bring those conditions to the surface. We cannot be responsible for damage.

You are having us perform this work at your own risk. By signing below you are releasing both this company and all parties working on your vehicle, and agree to hold all parties harmless for any damages, should damages occur.

Customer Signature_____

Date_____

Detailing Forums and Blogs

Autogeek
www.autogeekonline.net/forum/

Autopia
www.autopia.org

Auto Detailing Network
www.autodetailingnetwork.com

Detailing Success
www.detailingsuccess.com

Meguiar's Online
www.meguiarsonline.com

Detail Training, Learning, and Coaching

Detailing Success
www.detailingsuccess.com
Private one-on-one detail training and coaching.

Detail King
www.detailking.com
Group-based training that offers nice, entry-level training in the basics of detailing.

Industry Publications

Auto Detailing Magazine
www.autodetailingmag.com

Auto Detailing TV
www.autodetailingtv.com

Auto Laundry News
www.carwashmag.com

Detailers Digest
www.detailers-digest.com

Professional Car Washing and Detailing Magazine
www.carwash.com

Online Business Resources

IRS (www.irs.gov)
Great Information on forming a business and free resources.

SCORE (www.score.org)
SCORE mentors deliver FREE, confidential, valuable advice for your business needs. Whether you are a start-up or an existing business, our mentors will help you reach customers and achieve your goals.

Bill Myers Online (www.bmeyers.com)
Bill is a great guy to learn general business, marketing and sales from and his site has given me many good ideas over the years for my photo and video efforts alike.

Online Detailing Suppliers

Autogeek
www.autogeek.net

Auto Detailing Solutions
www.autodetailingsolutions.net

Glossary

This book is all about how to start a detailing business and not how to detail. But I am a chronic detailer and I believe there are many words and/or terms you need to be aware of. Below you have a long list of common terms from within the industry. Some are pretty old school while others are newer. Don't freak out and go on an all-out challenge to memorize these terms as you will most like only use about half of them right off the bat. Over the duration of your detailing career, you will come across all of them and then some.

Abrasive: Natural or synthetic particles (grit or media) found in polishes or compounds that cut the paint surface to remove imperfections.

Accelerated Paint Finishes: Refinish work placed in an environment with an air make-up system that accelerates the drying time from four hours to approximately one.

Acid: A substance below 7 on the pH scale. Different types of acid include phosphoric, sulfuric, oxalic and hydrofluoric. Mainly used in wheel cleaners.

Acid Rain: Rain contaminated with acidic compounds from industrial pollution. May cause damage to automotive finishes and glass.

Adhesion: How well a product bonds to the surface.

Alkaline-Alkalis: Substances above 9 on the pH scale, classified as basic or caustic. Caustic compounds are used in cleaning products such as soaps.

Base Coat: The foundation layer in the base coat/clear coat automotive finishes.

Bath Tub Mixer: A slang term used to refer to a manufacturer who mixes his/her own chemical products in a large drum. This level of product is usually at a low price and is of terrible quality.

Biodegradable: Capable of being broken down into safe, stable sub-compounds by natural forces.

Body Shop Safe: A term used to refer to products for body shops that contain no silicone or wax components that interfere with the painting system.

Buffer: A piece of equipment used by detailing technicians to correct paint or apply products to a vehicle (polisher).

Buffer(ing) Marks: Marks left by aggressive techniques, aggressive foam, and/or wool cutting pads used by an inexperienced detailer.

Burn: Damage to paint surface by a polisher or by aggressive sanding.

Cleaner/Glaze: Combination of a light abrasive cleaner and other products that clean and shine in one single step. Many times it has fillers, so the correction is temporary. *NOTE:* Some products have the word "Glaze" within their trade name but in reality, the product does not have fillers.

Cleaner/Wax: Combination of a light abrasive, various chemicals, and waxes that allow the user to clean, shine, and provide protection in one step.

Clear Coat: A thin transparent layer of paint (enamel or lacquer based) applied over a pigmented layer of paint (the base coat) to provide a high-gloss finish.

Compound/Compounding: An abrasive (liquid or paste) product designed to remove oxidation, scratches, and other imperfections. The first step in the detail process.

Compound Scratches/Swirls: Scratches in the painted finish due to abrasives in compounds and buffing cleaners as well as cutting pads.

Concentrate: A product that requires thinning with water or a reducer of one type or another.

Conventional Paint: More traditional ways of finishing automotive surfaces. Generally recognized as lacquered, acrylic, enamel, and acrylic/enamel paint finishes.

Cosmoline: A heavy-grade petroleum by-product or paraffin chemical applied to automobile exteriors as a protective coating during the transportation of the new vehicle. Removing this product can require special chemicals and procedures.

Checking, Cracking, and Crazing: Paint many times looks like shattered glass or brittle old window glass. Extreme temperatures cause the paint to expand and contract and pulls the paint apart at weak points. Also common when a car has egg and/or bird droppings on the surface.

Cutting Pad: Most often a wool pad with fibrous strands that resemble twisted carpet. May also be coarse foam pads such as many common yellow-foam pads.

Detergents: Cleaning products for auto interiors and exteriors with different chemical formulations as the active cleaning agent.

Dilute: To reduce by thinning with water. Always dilute in accordance with directions provided.

Dressing: Water-based and solvent-based liquids designed to provide protection and/or gloss to vinyl, plastic, and leather.

Dry Sanding: An alternative to wet sanding and a system I prefer on factory paint (OEM, Original Equipment Manufacturer).

Durability: The long-term resistance to the elements.

Dwell Time: During cleaning, a product may be required to sit, or dwell, for several minutes before being rinsed.

Enamel Paint: Type of OEM paint used for many years.

EPA: Environmental Protection Agency. A government agency that oversees many aspects of items that are dealt with in regard to the environment.

Extractor: A machine used to clean carpet and cloth seats. Applies cleaning solution in fan spray and removes moisture and dirt with vacuum action.

Fabric Guard: A product applied to fabric or cloth seats and carpets to repel soil and stains.

Finishing Pad: A soft foam pad made for finishing. Each manufacturer has various colors of foam for this purpose.

Fish Eye Within The Paint: Paint defects that are embedded during the painting process caused by dust, oil or other deposits that are left on the painted surface during the painting process.

Flash Point: The temperature at which a product when heated, will release a combustible vapor.

Forced-Action Polisher: This polisher not only orbits but it also rotates too, at the same time. A very capable polisher for paint correction and finish work alike.

Glaze: Product designed to produce a quick, high shine with little durability and fillers that fills in voids on a temporary basis.

Hazardous Chemicals: Chemicals that can pose a health risk to the user if used improperly or if proper safety equipment is not used. Read the MSDS (Material Safety Data Sheets) for each product you use. Warnings are normally written as if hazardous product were at 100 percent solution.

High-Temp Finishes: OEM paint finishes that are baked at a temperature of 260 to 300 degrees Fahrenheit for 30 to 60 minutes.

Industrial Fallout: Airborne pollutants from heavy industry or railroads which settle onto automotive surfaces and become embedded in the finish. Gradually, the particles oxidize and appear as dark specks in the paint. Requires special products and procedures to be removed.

MSDS: Material Safety Data Sheet. Standardized sheet that systematically describes a product and its hazardous chemical components. Distributors are to provide customers with a MSDS sheet for every product they buy. Distributors should also have a full set of MSDS sheets on their truck.

Metallic: An automotive color that has a glittery or metal-looking appearance.

Metering System: A way to mix chemicals with water as we use them within our detailing businesses. These systems mix at a precise level, saving us money on wasted products.

Multiple-Step Process: When two or more polishing steps are performed to properly process the painted surfaces of the vehicle.

OSHA (Occupational Safety and Health Administration): Government agency that sets standards for workplace safety.

One Step: Polishing a vehicle with one product that both cleans and seals at the same time. Sometimes used as shortcut to speed production of dealers' vehicles.

Orange Peel: The rough, uneven appearance of paint that resembles the surface of an orange or golfball that at one time was only witnessed on repaints. Now, 90 percent of new vehicles' finishes are covered in orange peel.

Orbital Buffer: A buffer with a pad that travels ellipses instead of rotating rotationally.

Original Finish: The paint finish applied by the vehicle manufacturer.

Overspray: Paints, stains, or other substances that settle out of the air onto automobile surface appearing as small, hard to remove speckles.

Oxidation: Loss of nutrients in the paint due to exposure such as sun, salt air, and adverse weather. The surface appears to have a chalky or dull look to it.

Pad Washer: A mechanical device used to remove accumulations of compounds and cleaners from buffing pads. Uses water spray and spur action while the pad is on the buffer.

Paint Sealer: A product applied to a clean surface to protect the paint. Durability and degree of gloss will vary greatly.

Paint Thickness: The amount of paint film on the vehicle. Measured in microns or millimeters.

Petroleum Distillates: Compounds that are derived from petroleum through the refining process that are used as additives within detailing products.

pH Scale: A scale used to determine the nature of water-soluble chemicals. 0–6 acid; 7–8 neutral; 9–14 alkaline–caustic.

Polisher: A piece of equipment used by skilled technicians to apply products to the painted surface of a vehicle. Typically turn at 600 to 3000 RPM.

Polymer: A synthetic substance made up of large molecules formed by smaller molecules of the same substance with a definite mission to protect painted and or non-painted surfaces. These items can be found within the production of today's most durable waxes and sealers.

Pre-Wash: First step in preparing a vehicle for detailing many times found in the form or foam.

PSI (Pounds Per Square Inch): A measure of air and water pressure and most commonly found within detailing on both pressure washers and air compressors.

RPM: Revolutions Per Minute; number of complete turns made in one minute. This term is most commonly used within detailing for gauging the speed of a rotational polisher.

Rail Dust: Small metallic particles attributed to railroads which settle onto automotive surfaces and become embedded in the finish. These particles can oxidize and appear as dark or red specks in the paint surface and can require special products and/or procedures to remove.

Re-Flow Technique: A system during paint correction where light to heavy imperfections are filled with surrounding clear coat.

Sealant: A protective product that penetrates surface to bond with existing paint finish. Polymer resins create a protective film much more durable than wax. Subject to the same elements but with much more longevity.

Silicate: A hard glossy compound usually some form of the dioxide of silicone and used within the manufacturing of waxes, polishes, and compounds.

Solvent: A substance, usually liquid, that dissolves or can dissolve another substance.

Steamer: A newer tool for using within both interiors and exteriors within the detailing trade.

Swirl Marks: Same as buffer marks but due generally to application of pressure.

Teflon: Nonstick coating to reduce surface friction. Teflon powder may be used in sealers and waxes. Not my favorite material for this purpose, by the way.

Two Step: A term to describe the process of cleaning or polishing the paint surface followed by a separate finishing application of a durable coating of wax or sealer.

UV Rays: UV rays is the major cause and reason that deteriorates automobile surfaces and can cause fading, cracking, peeling, and discoloration to nearly all exposed surfaces of the average automobile. Some products contain UV blockers and basically act as sunscreen for your car.

Water Based: A chemical whose primary liquid ingredient is water.

Wet Sanding: This is a system used for the smoothing or enhancement of a repaint, or in our case as detailers, as a way to remove paint blemishes.

Index

About the Author

Renny Doyle has been a Master Detailer for over thirty years and his list of clientele is filled with business leaders and celebrities alike. Renny had humble beginnings within the detail industry and has built his businesses based on the sound business, marketing, and sales principles that have supported his growth and success within the detailing industry.

Renny is the "Detailer of Air Force One" and has worked on, and cosmetically restored, both automobiles and aircraft at the collector and museum levels for the past decade. As part of those projects, he and his wife Diane run www.detailersofairforceone.com and www.detailingsuccess.com.

In addition, Renny coaches, trains, and mentors new and experienced detailers from across the globe within a one-on-one coaching environment at his detailing studio in Southern California and via his website and blog, www.detailingsuccess.com.

Renny is the editor of *Auto Detailing Magazine* and the producer of www.AutoDetailingTV.com.

Renny and his wife are the proud parents of four wonderful children, and their family resides in a resort community just outside of Los Angeles, California.